KÖNEMANN

© 2015 for this edition: koenemann.com GmbH

Distributed in cooperation with Frechmann Kolón GmbH

www.koenemann.com

www.frechmann.com

Published in the United States in 2016 by:

Skyhorse Publishing

307 West 36th Street, 11th Floor

New York, NY 10018, USA

T: +1 212 643 6816

info@skyhorsepublishing.com

www.skyhorsepublishing.com

Editorial project: LOFT Publications

Barcelona, Spain

Tel.: +34 932 688 088

Fax: +34 932 687 073

loft@loftpublications.com

www.loftpublications.com

Editorial coordination: Claudia Martínez Alonso

Assistant editorial coordination: Ana Marques

Editor and Texts: Marta Serrats

Edition assistant: Alejandra Muñoz Solano

Art director: Mireia Casanovas Soley

Layout: Jaume Martínez Coscpjuela

Translations: textcase

ISBN 978-3-86407-417-2 (GB)

ISBN 978-3-86407-415-8 (D)

ISBN 978-3-86407-416-5 (E)

ISBN 978-1-5107-0451-0 (Skyhorse, USA)

Printed in Spain

NATURAL BATHROOMS

SALLES DE BAINS NATURELLES

NATÜRLICHE BÄDER

NATUURLIJKE BADKAMERS

BAÑOS NATURALES

BAGNI NATURALI

BANHEIROS NATURAIS

NATURLIGA BADRUM

New bathrooms strive for a natural sensuality, and materials like stone and wood are in vogue for helping this room to awaken our senses.

There are many materials designed for the bathroom that are adapted to the rigors of everyday life and intended to dominate the overall aesthetics of this space. However, the result is not always what was expected, as they can be unattractive or even unsubstantial. Materials like chrome and acrylic are ideal for fixtures, but they should be complemented by other more organic and tactile ones to create a balanced appearance.

Bathroom suites built with ceramic, stone, resin or other natural materials are an ideal choice for creating a space that is conducive to relaxation. In recent years, bathroom furniture has relied heavily on these types of high-quality materials. Consumers have opted for a natural wood finish for their furnishings, whether it be light-coloured woods like oak and pine, or darker tones such as walnut or *wenge*. These features exude a passion for naturalness and convey warm sensations to users while also conforming to the style of modern architecture. This type of material combines perfection with a light and transparent bathroom architecture.

Other materials like stone and glass combine to create a very natural atmosphere in the bathroom. Stone sinks and bathtubs continue this trend and introduce a unique, refined character to any décor. Wooden accessories give contemporary bathrooms a casual air, while crystal tiling adds a majestic touch to the home.

Sustainability is coupled with a timeless design, for example, in the case of companies that use vitreous enamelled steel, which comes directly from natural sources and can be completely recycled when the products are no longer used.

Die neuen Bäder bestechen durch eine natürliche Sinnlichkeit. Materialien wie Holz und Stein werden aktuell dazu verwendet, während des Aufenthalts im Bad unsere Sinne zu beleben.

Es gibt viele speziell auf das Bad zugeschnittene Materialien, die sich in das tägliche Leben einfügen und sogar eigens dazu entwickelt wurden, eine allgemeine Ästhetik zu schaffen. Dennoch ist das Ergebnis nicht immer wie erwartet, da sie wenig ansehnlich oder steril wirken können. Materialien wie Chrom und Acryl sind ideal für die Armaturen, sie müssen jedoch mit etwas mehr organischem und taktilem verbunden werden, um einen ausgeglichenen Anblick zu bieten.

Badzubehör aus Keramik, Stein, Harz und anderen natürlichen Materialien ist ideal, um einen Ort zu schaffen, der zum Entspannen einlädt. In den letzten Jahren werden Badezimmermöbel stark aus diesen edlen Materialien dominiert. Bei der Verarbeitung der Möbel entscheidet man sich gewöhnlich für ein natürliches Holz. Dies können helle Hölzer wie Eiche oder Kiefer oder dunkle wie Nussbaum oder *Wenge* sein. Diese strahlen eine Leidenschaft für das Natürliche aus und wirken beruhigend auf den Benutzer, während sie sich gleichzeitig hervorragend in die neue Architektur einfügen. Diese Materialien kombinieren Perfektion mit klarer und transparenter Badarchitektur.

Um eine natürliche Atmosphäre im Badezimmer zu schaffen, werden Materialien wie Stein und Glas verwendet. Steinwaschbecken und -badewannen setzen einen Trend fort und verleihen jeder Dekoration einen einzigartigen und feinen Charakter. Holzaccessoires geben zeitgemäßen Bädern eine lässige Ausstrahlung, während Glasfliesen dem Raum einen majestätischen Touch verleihen.

Nachhaltigkeit geht einher mit einem zeitgemäßen Design. Dies zeigt sich am Beispiel einiger Firmen, die dicken, verglasten Stahl verwenden, der direkt aus der Natur kommt und, wenn die Lebenszeit des Produkts abgelaufen ist, hundertfach recycelt wird.

Les nouvelles salles de bains font la part belle à une sensualité naturelle. Les matériaux tels que la pierre et le bois sont particulièrement prisés dans la salle de bains afin d'obtenir un espace qui mette nos sens en éveil.

Il existe de nombreux matériaux spécialement conçus pour la salle de bains, à même de s'adapter aux rigueurs d'un usage quotidien et pensés pour dominer l'esthétique d'ensemble de cet espace. Cependant, il n'est pas toujours possible d'obtenir le résultat attendu car ces matériaux peuvent perdre de leur attrait au point d'en devenir insignifiants. Les matériaux comme le chrome et l'acrylique sont parfaits pour la robinetterie mais il est fondamental de les associer avec des matériaux plus organiques et tactiles qui permettent d'instaurer un ensemble équilibré.

Les salles de bains composées de céramique, de pierre, de résine ou d'autres matériaux naturels sont un choix idéal pour obtenir un espace qui invite à la détente. Cela fait quelques années que le mobilier de salles de bains est essentiellement produit dans ce type de matériaux nobles. Pour les finitions des meubles, on opte pour un aspect bois naturel, qu'il s'agisse de bois clairs tels que le chêne et le pin ou de bois plus sombres tels que le noyer et le wengé. Ces matériaux dénotent une réelle passion pour tout ce qui est naturel et apportent une touche chaleureuse aux espaces tout en s'adaptant au langage de l'architecture moderne. Ce type de matériaux se combine à la perfection avec une architecture de salles de bains claire et fluide.

D'autres matériaux comme la pierre et le verre peuvent être associés afin de créer une ambiance très naturelle dans la salle de bains. Les lavabos et les baignoires en pierre sont toujours très recherchés et donnent un cachet unique et raffiné, quel que soit le cadre. Les accessoires en bois donnent un côté casual aux salles de bains aux lignes contemporaines, tandis que les carreaux de verre apportent une touche majestueuse à la pièce.

La durabilité est indissociable d'un design intemporel. C'est pourquoi certaines entreprises utilisent de l'acier émaillé vitrifié, un matériau totalement naturel et cent pour cent recyclable lorsque les produits ne sont plus utilisés.

De nieuwste badkamers wekken veel belangstelling op. Met populaire materialen als natuursteen en hout prikkelen ze onze zinnen.

Voor de badkamer zijn talrijke materialen ontworpen die geschikt zijn voor het dagelijks gebruik van deze ruimte en tegelijkertijd fungeren als esthetische smaakmaker. Toch is het resultaat niet altijd zoals verwacht en pakt de badkamer soms niet erg aantrekkelijk of zelfs steriel uit. Materialen als chroom en kunststoffen zijn ideaal voor kranen en dergelijke, maar voor een evenwichtige uitstraling is compensatie in de vorm van meer organische en tactiele materialen noodzakelijk.

Om van een badkamer een ontspannende ruimte te maken, zijn keramiek, natuursteen, hars en andere natuurlijke materialen uitermate geschikt. De laatste jaren is er dan ook een sterke trend om het badkamermeubilair uit dergelijke materialen te vervaardigen. Voor de afwerking van de meubels wordt vaak een natuurlijke hout-*look* toegepast, hetzij licht, van eiken- of dennenhout, hetzij donker, van notenhout of wengé. Zo worden gebruikers aangenaam getroffen door het natuurlijk en warme karakter van de badkamer en is er tegelijkertijd sprake van moderne architectuur. Deze materialen passen perfect in een licht en transparant badkamerontwerp.

Andere materialen als natuursteen en glas worden gebruikt om in de badkamer een natuurlijke sfeer te creëren. Natuurstenen wasfels en badkuipen komen steeds vaker voor en drukken een uniek en verfijnd stempel op de inrichting. Houten accessoires geven een badkamer in een hedendaagse lijnvoering iets "casuals", terwijl glazen tegels het vertrek een majestueuze toets geven.

Dat duurzaamheid hand in hand kan gaan met een tijdloos ontwerp bewijzen sommige bedrijven die dik geëmailleerd staal gebruiken, dat direct uit de natuur komt en dat voor honderd procent kan worden gerecycled.

Los nuevos baños apuestan por una sensualidad natural, y los materiales como la piedra y la madera están de moda para que esta estancia despierte nuestros sentidos.

Existen numerosos materiales diseñados para el baño que se adaptan a los rigores de la vida diaria, e incluso que han sido pensados para dominar la estética general de este espacio. Sin embargo, el resultado no es siempre el esperado, porque pueden llegar a ser poco atractivos y hasta resultar un poco estériles. Los materiales como el cromo y el acrílico son ideales para la grifería, pero es necesario compensarlos con otros más orgánicos y táctiles que permitan una mirada equilibrada.

Las suites de baño fabricadas con cerámica, piedra, resina u otros materiales naturales son una apuesta ideal para lograr un espacio que invite al relax. En los últimos años, el mobiliario de baño apuesta fuerte por este tipo de materiales nobles. Para los acabados de los muebles se opta por un aspecto de madera natural, ya sean maderas claras como el roble y el pino, o tonos más oscuros como el nogal y el *wengué*. Estos materiales irradian su pasión por la naturalidad y envían cálidas señales a los usuarios a la vez que se adaptan al lenguaje de la arquitectura moderna. Este tipo de materiales combina a la perfección con una arquitectura de baño clara y transparente.

Otros materiales como la piedra y el vidrio se combinan para crear una atmósfera muy natural en el cuarto de baño. Los lavamanos y las bañeras de piedra continúan en tendencia e imprimen un carácter único y refinado a cualquier decoración. Los accesorios en madera dan un aire *casual* a los baños de líneas contemporáneas, mientras que los azulejos de cristal agregan un toque majestuoso a la habitación.

La sostenibilidad va unida a un diseño atemporal, como en el caso de algunas firmas que emplean acero grueso vitrificado que proviene directamente de la naturaleza y se recicla al cien por cien cuando los productos dejan de utilizarse.

I nuovi bagni puntano su una sensualità naturale, e utilizzano i materiali come la pietra e il legno per fare risvegliare i nostri sensi.

Esistono numerosi materiali progettati per il bagno che si adattano al rigore della vita quotidiana, e che sono stati addirittura pensati per dominare l'estetica complessiva di questo spazio. Tuttavia, non sempre il risultato è quello sperato, perché possono diventare poco attraenti e risultare perfino un po' sterili. I materiali come il cromo e l'acrilico sono ideali per la rubinetteria, ma è necessario bilanciarli con altri più organici e tattili che consentano una visione equilibrata.

Gli arredi da bagno fabbricati in ceramica, pietra, resina o altri materiali naturali sono una scommessa ideale per ottenere uno spazio che inviti al relax. Negli ultimi anni, i mobili da bagno stanno puntando molto su questo tipo di materiali nobili. Per le finiture dei mobili si preferisce un aspetto di legno naturale, sia con legni chiari come il rovere o il pino, o con toni più scuri come il noce o il *wengé*. Questi trasmettono la loro passione per la natura ed emanano sensazioni di calore a chi li usa, adattandosi allo stesso tempo al linguaggio dell'architettura moderna. Questo tipo di materiali si combina perfettamente con un'architettura da bagno chiara e trasparente.

Altri materiali come la pietra e il vetro si combinano per dare vita ad un'atmosfera molto naturale nella stanza da bagno. I lavabi e le vasche da bagno in pietra sono ancora di moda e attribuiscono un carattere unico e raffinato a qualsiasi arredamento. Gli accessori di legno danno un'aria *casual* ai bagni dalle linee contemporanee, mentre le piastrelle di vetro aggiungono un tocco di maestosità alla stanza.

La sostenibilità si unisce al design senza tempo, come nel caso di alcune marche che utilizzano acciaio grezzo vetrificato che proviene direttamente dalla natura e viene riciclato al cento per cento quando i prodotti non sono più utilizzati.

Os novos banheiros apostam numa sensualidade natural e os materiais como a pedra e a madeira estão na moda, fazendo com que esta parte da casa desperte os nossos sentidos.

No entanto, o resultado nem sempre é o esperado e pode por vezes ser pouco atraente e revelar-se até um pouco estéril. Os materiais como os cromados e os acrílicos são ideais para as torneiras, mas é necessário compensá-los com outros mais orgânicos e táteis que permitam equilibrar o conjunto.

Os conjuntos de banheiro fabricados em cerâmica, pedra, resina ou outros materiais constituem uma aposta ideal para conseguir um espaço que convide ao relaxamento. De fato, nos últimos anos, o mobiliário de banheiro tem apostado decididamente nestes materiais nobres. Em relação ao acabamento dos móveis prefere-se o aspecto da madeira natural, seja ela clara, como o carvalho e o pinho, ou de tons mais escuros, como a nogueira e o vengué. São materiais que irradiam paixão pelo natural e enviam aos seus utilizadores uma sensação de aconchego, adaptando-se, ao mesmo tempo, à linguagem da arquitetura moderna. Este tipo de materiais combina com perfeição com uma arquitetura clara e transparente do banheiro.

Outros materiais, como a pedra e o vidro, combinam-se para criar uma atmosfera muito natural no banheiro. Os lavatórios e banheiras em pedra continuam na moda e imprimem um caráter único e refinado a qualquer decoração. Os acessórios em madeira emprestam um ar *casual* aos banheiros de linhas contemporâneas, ao passo que os mosaicos de vidro lhe conferem um toque majestoso.

A sustentabilidade pode aliar-se a um *design* intemporal, como no caso de algumas firmas que utilizam um aço vitrificado grosseiro, diretamente proveniente da natureza, que é cem por cento reciclável quando os produtos deixam de ser utilizados.

I nya badrum satsar man ofta på naturlig sensualitet, och material som sten och trä är på modet för att de väcker våra sinnen.

Det finns många material som är särskilt avsedda för badrum och som anpassats efter vardagspåfrestningarna, och kanske även är tänkta att dominera rummets allmänna utseende. Emellertid blir resultatet inte alltid som väntat, eftersom de kan kännas oattraktiva och lite sterila. Material som krom och akryl är idealiska för blandare, men det måste nästan vägas upp med mer organiska och känsliga material som ger ett balanserat utseende.

Badrumsserier i keramik, sten, harts eller andra naturmaterial är perfekta för att ge ett rum som inbjuder till avkoppling. Under de senaste åren har badrumsinredningarna gått över mer och mer till denna typ av ädla material. Som ytfinish väljer man ofta naturligt trä, antingen i ljusa träslag som ek och furu eller mörkare nyanser som valnöt och *wenge*. De avspeglar en passion för naturen och ger användaren ett intryck av värme samtidigt som de passar in i det moderna arkitektoniska språket. Sådana material kombinerar perfektion med en ljus och transparent badrumsarkitektur.

Andra material, som sten och glas, kan kombineras för att skapa en mycket naturlig atmosfär i badrummet. Trenden med handfat och badkar i sten fortsätter och ger en unik och raffinerad karaktär. Tillbehör i trä ger en avslappnad känsla i badrum med moderna linjer, medan glaskakel ger en majestätisk touch.

Hållbarhet går hand i hand med den tidlösa designen, som att vissa företag använder tjockt emaljerat stål som kommer direkt från naturen och kan återvinnas fullständigt när produkterna inte längre används.

11

17

TIPS

© DURAT

© DURAT

Choose materials with a low environmental impact, such as cork, coir and bamboo, or furniture made from recycled materials.

Opta por materiales que tengan un bajo impacto ambiental, como el corcho, el coco o el bambú, o por muebles realizados con materiales reciclables.

Choisissez des matériaux ayant un impact environnemental limité tels que le liège, le cocotier ou le bambou, ou des meubles en matériaux recyclables.

Scegli materiali che presentino un basso impatto ambientale, come il sughero, il cocco o il bambù, o mobili realizzati con materiali riciclabili.

Entscheiden Sie sich für Materialien, die wenig Einfluss auf die Umwelt haben, wie Kork, Kokos oder Bambus, oder für Möbel aus recycelbaren Materialien.

Opte por materiais com baixo impacto ambiental, como a cortiça, o coco e o bambu, ou por móveis construídos com materiais recicláveis.

Kies voor materialen die het milieu zo min mogelijk belasten, zoals kurk, kokos en bamboe, of voor meubels van hergebruikt materiaal.

Välj material som har en låg miljöpåverkan, som kork, kokos eller bambu, eller möbler tillverkade av återvinningsbart material.

51

STONE FOREST

Wooden sinks may be installed on any type of countertop or built into it.

Los lavamanos de madera pueden instalarse sobre cualquier tipo de encimera o integrarse en ella.

Il est possible d'installer un lavabo en bois sur n'importe quel type de surface, voire de l'y intégrer.

I lavandini in legno possono essere installati su qualsiasi tipo di piano o esservi inseriti.

Holzwaschbecken können auf jeder Oberfläche angebracht oder in sie integriert werden.

Os lavatórios em madeira podem ser instalados sobre qualquer tipo de base ou integrar-se nela.

Houten waskommen kunnen op of in elk type blad worden geïnstalleerd.

Tvättställ i trä kan monteras på alla typer av bänkar eller integreras i en bänk.

54

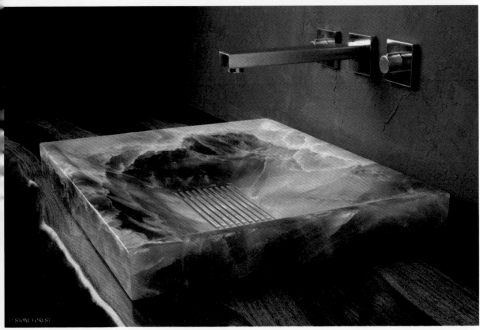

© BOXART

© DURAT

Use fine materials in the bathroom as an aesthetic solution. They provide quality and evoke nature.

Apuesta por el empleo de materiales nobles en el baño como una solución estética. Aportan calidez y remiten a la naturaleza.

Pour la décoration de votre salle de bains, optez pour des matériaux nobles. Ils apportent une touche chaleureuse et naturelle.

Punta sull'utilizzo di materiali nobili nel bagno come soluzione estetica. Attribuiscono calore e rievocano la natura.

Verwenden Sie hochwertige Materialien, um eine ästhetische Lösung zu finden. Sie bringen Wärme und Natürlichkeit.

Aposte na utilização de materiais nobres no banheiro como solução estética, pois transmitem calor e remetem para a natureza.

Verhoog de esthetiek in de badkamer met edele materialen. Ze zorgen voor een warme en natuurlijke uitstraling.

Satsa på material av hög kvalitet i badrummet som en estetisk lösning. De bidrar med en varm och naturlig känsla.

© CERAMICA FLAMINIA

© PORCELANOSA GRUPO

Fill the bathroom with items and furnishings made with natural raw materials and in organic colours. You can also reuse objects, giving them a new purpose.

Llena el baño con complementos y muebles realizados con materias primas naturales y de colores orgánicos. También puedes reutilizar objetos dándoles un nuevo uso.

Ornez votre salle de bains d'accessoires et de meubles en matières premières naturelles et de couleurs organiques. Vous pouvez aussi recycler des objets en les utilisant d'une autre manière.

Riempi il bagno di accessori e mobili realizzati con materie prime naturali e dai colori biologici. Puoi anche riutilizzare gli oggetti assegnando loro un nuovo uso.

Füllen Sie das Bad mit Accessoires und Möbeln in organischen Farben, die mit Rohstoffen in Verbindung gebracht werden. Sie können auch alte Objekte neu verwenden.

Use no banheiro acessórios e móveis construídos com matérias-primas naturais e de cores orgânicas. Pode também reutilizar objetos, dando-lhes um novo uso.

Richt de badkamer in met meubels en accessoires van natuurlijke grondstoffen en in levendige kleuren. Ook kunt u voorwerpen hergebruiken door ze een nieuwe bestemming te geven.

Fyll badrummet med tillbehör och möbler i naturmaterial och ekologiska färger. Du kan också återanvända föremål på nya sätt.

© TAU CERÁMICA

> STONE FOREST

© BOXART

Birch is very well suited to this type of room, as it reduces capacity for absorption of moisture as a result of a high-temperature process that changes its chemical composition.

El abedul es muy apropiado para este tipo de piezas, porque reduce la capacidad de absorción de humedad gracias a un proceso de alta temperatura que cambia su composición química.

Le bouleau convient bien à ce type de pièces car c'est un matériau doté d'une capacité d'absorption de l'humidité limitée grâce à un traitement à haute température qui modifie sa composition chimique.

La betulla è particolarmente adatta per questo tipo di elementi, perché riduce la capacità di assorbire l'umidità grazie a un proceso di alta temperatura che cambia la sua composizione chimica.

Birke ist hier sehr geeignet, da sie aufgrund der hohen Temperaturen, die benötigt werden, um ihre chemische Zusammensetzung zu verändern, die Aufnahme von Feuchtigkeit reduziert.

A bétula é muito apropriada para este tipo de divisões, porque reduz a capacidade de absorção de humidade, graças a um proceso a altas temperaturas que altera a sua composição química.

Berkenhout is zeer geschikt voor dit soort ruimtes omdat het minder vocht opneemt nadat het is bewerkt onder hoge temperatuur, waarbij de chemische samenstelling is veranderd.

Björk är mycket lämpligt för denna typ av föremål, eftersom fuktupptagningsförmågan kan sänkas med hjälp av en värmebehandling som förändrar dess kemiska sammansättning.

SMART BATHROOMS

SALLES DE BAINS INTELLIGENTES

INTELLIGENTE BÄDER

SLIMME BADKAMERS

BAÑOS INTELIGENTES

BAGNI INTELLIGENTI

BANHEIROS INTELIGENTES

SMARTA BADRUM

In the bathroom, every drop counts. Bathroom design is going green, incorporating new codes in pursuit of responsible care for the environment. Reduction of water from the tank, recycling of water used by the shower, use of low-energy LED lighting and decoration with natural elements are some of the measures being taken in the design of this type of smart bathroom.

Many of the technological advances occurring in the past few years have led to significant improvements in comfort, hygiene and energy efficiency. With regard to reduction of water consumption, there are smart showers with sensors that make it possible to conserve water by pointing the stream in the exact position where the person is located, which serves to avoid unnecessary waste. Water-saving showerheads can also be installed, which reduce the flow of water by combining it with hot air. If an LED lighting system is used, the colour of the water will change according to the temperature or individual tastes when the person is bathing.

Advances in engineering and home automation have also revolutionized so-called smart toilets, which include all the functions of the bidet and are programmable and adjustable. They include self-cleaning and automatic closing systems that produce minimal noise during this process. Hygiene and comfort are guaranteed when using this toilet, which includes a heating system for the seat and hot air jets for the feet.

In terms of furniture, consumers can opt for touch-screen mirrors that include music, radio, Internet and even television programming systems. Some are designed to make life easier for seniors, with simple programs built into the mirror to remind users to do anything from brushing their teeth to taking their medication.

Im Bad zählt jeder Tropfen. Der ökologische Aspekt steht im Gegensatz zum Design des Bades und bedient sich daher neuer Möglichkeiten, den umweltbewussten Bürger anzusprechen. Verringerung des Wasserverbrauchs bei der Toilettenspülung, Wasserrecycling für die Dusche, LED-Lampen zum Energiesparen und Dekoration mit natürlichen Elementen gehören zu den Komponenten, die verstärkt für diese intelligenten Bäder eingesetzt werden.

Viele der technischen Fortschritte der vergangenen Jahre haben deutliche Verbesserungen bei Komfort, Hygiene und Energieeffizienz mit sich gebracht. Zum Wassersparen gibt es intelligente Duschköpfe, die es dank ihrer Sensoren schaffen, den Strahl genau auf den Duschenden zu richten, was unnötige Verluste vermeidet. Ebenso können Wasserperlatoren eingesetzt werden, die den Wasserstrahl verringern, indem sie ihn mit warmer Luft kombinieren. Wird ein LED-System eingebaut, so ändert sich die Wasserfarbe mit der Temperatur oder gemäß den eigenen Wünschen beim Baden.

Die Fortschritte in der Ingenieur- und Haustechnik haben auch die so genannten intelligenten Toiletten revolutioniert. Diese haben nun auch alle Funktionen eines Bidets und sind programmier- und regulierbar. Sie enthalten Systeme zur automatischen Reinigung sowie zum automatischen Verschließen, die ein langsames Absenken ermöglichen. Toilettenhygiene und -komfort werden durch Sitzheizung und warme Luftströme an den Füßen garantiert.

Bei den Möbeln kann man sich für taktile Spiegel entscheiden, mit denen man Musik, Radio, Internet und sogar Fernsehen nutzen kann. Manche zielen darauf ab, älteren Menschen das Leben zu erleichtern. Hier sind einfache Programme in die Spiegel eingebaut, die daran erinnern, die Zähne zu putzen oder seine Medikamente einzunehmen.

Dans la salle de bains, chaque goutte d'eau compte. La pensée écologique infiltre le design des salles de bains et y intègre de nouveaux codes dans sa recherche d'une approche responsable de la protection de l'environnement. Réduire le volume d'eau de la chasse d'eau, recycler l'eau de la douche, utiliser des lampes LED à basse consommation et opter pour des éléments de décoration naturels sont quelques-uns des éléments aujourd'hui incontournables de ce type de salles de bains intelligentes.

Les nombreux progrès technologiques réalisés ces dernières années ont permis d'améliorer grandement le confort, l'hygiène et l'efficacité énergétique. En matière d'économies d'eau, il existe des pommes de douche intelligents qui permettent, grâce à des capteurs, d'économiser l'eau en adaptant le jet exactement à la position dans laquelle vous vous trouvez, ce qui évite un gaspillage inutile. En outre, il est possible d'installer des aérateurs sur les robinets afin de diminuer le débit d'eau en le combinant avec de l'air chaud. Si vous disposez d'un système d'éclairage LED, la couleur de l'eau changera en fonction de la température ou de vos goûts personnels au moment de prendre un bain.

Les progrès en ingénierie et en domotique ont également révolutionné les toilettes dites intelligentes qui intègrent de multiples fonctions et sont programmables et réglables. Elles comprennent notamment des systèmes d'auto-nettoyage et de fermeture automatique qui permettent une descente amortie de l'abattant. L'hygiène et le confort aux toilettes sont assurés grâce à un système de chauffage de la lunette et un souffleur d'air chaud pour les pieds.

Quant au mobilier, il est possible de disposer de miroirs à écran tactile intégrant des systèmes de programmation musicale, la radio, Internet et même la télévision. Certains de ces systèmes sont conçus pour faciliter la vie aux personnes âgées dans la mesure où ils vont jusqu'à intégrer aux miroirs des programmes simples pour rappeler à ces personnes qu'elles doivent par exemple se laver les dents ou encore prendre certains médicaments.

In de badkamer telt elke druppel. Ook in het ontwerp van badkamers doet de ecologische benadering zijn intrede en worden manieren gezocht om milieuvriendelijk te werk te gaan. Minder spoelwater, hergebruik van douchewater, het gebruik van energiezuinige ledverlichting en een inrichting met natuurlijke elementen zijn slechts een paar voorbeelde n van een voortvarende nieuwe aanpak in slimme badkamers.

In de afgelopen jaren hebben veel technologische ontwikkelingen geleid tot aanzienlijke verbeteringen op het gebied van comfort, hygiëne en energiegebruik. Zo bestaan er bijvoorbeeld voor waterbesparing slimme douches die met behulp van sensoren de waterstraal precies op de degene die eronder staat kunnen richten en zo onnodig waterverlies voorkomen. Ook kunnen er op kranen mondstukken worden geïnstalleerd die de waterstroom vermengen met hete lucht en zo water besparen. Door ledverlichting te installeren kan de kleur van het water tijdens het baden op de persoonlijke smaak van de gebruiker worden afgestemd.

De vooruitgang op technisch gebied en dan met name binnen de domotica, heeft ook geleid tot intelligente toiletten met ingebouwde bidetfunctie, volledig programmeerbaar en regelbaar. Ze zijn zelfreinigend en voorzien van een automatisch gedempt sluitingsmechanisme. Ook aan het comfort van de toiletpot is gedacht: de bril is voorzien van een verwarmingssysteem en warmeluchtventielen zorgen voor de verwarming van de voeten.

Wat het meubilair betreft kunt u bijvoorbeeld kiezen voor een spiegel met aanraakscherm voor de bediening van de ingebouwde muziek-, radio-, internet- en zelfs televisiefunctie. Sommige zijn speciaal ontworpen voor oude mensen: de spiegel is dan voorzien van eenvoudige programma's die de gebruiker eraan herinneren dat hij zijn tanden moet poetsen en zijn medicijnen moet innemen.

En el baño cada gota cuenta. El espíritu ecológico invade el diseño de los baños e incorpora nuevos códigos en busca de un cuidado responsable del medio ambiente. La reducción del agua de la cisterna, el reciclaje del agua para la ducha, el uso de iluminación led de bajo consumo y la decoración con elementos naturales son algunas de las medidas que se están imponiendo con fuerza en las instalaciones de este tipo de baños inteligentes.

Muchos de los avances tecnológicos llevados a cabo en los últimos años han desembocado en sensibles mejoras en confort, higiene y eficiencia energética. Si de lo que se trata es de ahorrar agua, existen duchas inteligentes que permiten, gracias a sus sensores, economizarla apuntando el chorro exactamente en la posición donde se encuentra el individuo, lo que evita pérdidas innecesarias. Igualmente, se pueden instalar perlizadores para dispensar agua, que disminuyen el caudal combinándola con aire caliente. Si se incorpora un sistema de iluminación led, el color del agua cambiará en función de la temperatura o de los propios gustos en el momento de tomar el baño.

Los avances en ingeniería y domótica han revolucionado también los llamados inodoros inteligentes, que incorporan todas las funciones del bidé y son programables y regulables. Integran sistemas de autolimpieza y de cerramiento automático que permiten un cierre amortiguado. La higiene y la comodidad en el inodoro quedan garantizadas con sistemas de calefacción en el asiento y dispensadores de aire caliente para los pies.

En cuanto al mobiliario, se pueden optar por espejos de pantalla táctil que incorporan sistemas de programación musical, radio, Internet e incluso televisión. Algunos están diseñados para facilitar la vida a las personas mayores, pues incorporan programas sencillos integrados en el propio espejo para recordar desde la necesidad de lavarse los dientes hasta los medicamentos que hay que tomar.

Nel bagno ogni goccia conta. Lo spirito ecologico pervade il design dei bagni e ingloba nuovi codici alla ricerca di un'attenzione responsabile per l'ambiente. La riduzione dell'acqua della cassetta, il recupero dell'acqua per la doccia, l'utilizzo di illuminazione LED a basso consumo e l'arredamento con elementi naturali sono alcuni degli accorgimenti che si stanno imponendo con forza nell'installazione di questo tipo di bagni intelligenti.

Molti dei progressi tecnologici compiuti durante gli ultimi anni sono sfociati in netti miglioramenti nel comfort, igiene ed efficienza energetica. Se il fine è risparmiare acqua, esistono docce intelligenti che consentono, grazie ai loro sensori, di razionarla puntando il getto nell'esatta posizione in cui si trova l'individuo, così da evitare sprechi inutili. Allo stesso modo, è possibile installare economizzatori per dispensare acqua, che ne diminuiscono la portata combinandola con aria calda. Se si include un sistema di illuminazione LED, il colore dell'acqua cambierà in base alla temperatura o ai propri gusti nel momento in cui si fa il bagno.

I progressi nell'ingegneria e nella domotica hanno rivoluzionato anche i cosiddetti water intelligenti, che includono tutte le funzioni del bidet, programmabili e regolabili. Comprendono sistemi di pulizia e di chiusura automatica che consentono una chiusura attenuata. L'igiene e la comodità del water sono garantite da sistemi di riscaldamento della tavoletta e da dispensatori di aria calda per i piedi.

Per quanto riguarda i mobili, è possibile preferire specchi con touch screen che includono sistemi di programmazione musicale, radio, Internet e perfino televisione. Alcuni sono progettati per agevolare la vita agli anziani, infatti presentano programmi semplici integrati nello specchio stesso per ricordare varie necessità, da lavarsi i denti ai medicinali che occorre prendere.

No banheiro cada gota é importante. O espírito ecológico invade o *design* dos banheiros e introduz novos códigos, na busca de uma preocupação responsável com o ambiente. A redução da água do autoclismo, a reciclagem da água da ducha, o uso de iluminação LED de baixo consumo e a decoração com elementos naturais são algumas das medidas que se impõem com força na instalação deste tipo de banheiros inteligentes.

Muitos dos avanços tecnológicos conseguidos nos últimos anos conduziram a uma melhoria considerável nos níveis de conforto, higiene e eficiência energética. Quando se trata de poupar água, existem chuveiros inteligentes que permitem, por meio de sensores, reduzir o seu consumo, apontando o jato exatamente para a posição em que se encontra o utilizador, o que evita perdas desnecessárias. Podem igualmente instalar-se redutores, que diminuem o caudal da água, combinando-a com ar quente. Incorporando-lhe um sistema de iluminação LED, a cor da água pode variar durante o banho, em função da sua temperatura ou dos gostos pessoais.

Os avanços em engenharia e domótica revolucionaram igualmente as chamadas sanitários inteligentes, que desempenham todas as funções do bidé, de forma programável e regulável. Dispõem de sistemas de autolimpeza e fecho automático, que permitem um fecho suave. A higiene e a comodidade sanitária ficam garantidas graças aos sistemas de aquecimento do assento e dispensadores de ar quente para os pés.

Quanto ao mobiliário, é possível optar por espelhos de ecrã tátil com sistemas integrados de programação musical, rádio, Internet e até televisão. Alguns deles foram concebidos para facilitar a vida aos mais idosos, dispondo de programas simples integrados no próprio espelho que lhes recordam a necessidade de escovar os dentes e os medicamentos que têm de tomar.

I badrummet räknas varenda droppe. Den ekologiska andan har invaderat badrumsdesignen och medför nya vanor i jakten på större respekt för miljön. Minskad mängd vatten i cisternen, återanvändning av duschvatten, LED-belysning med låg elförbrukning och inredning med naturelement är några av de åtgärder som har kommit att utnyttjas mycket i inredningen av smarta badrum.

Många av de tekniska framstegen som kommit de senaste åren har resulterat i betydande förbättringar i komfort, hygien och energieffektivitet. Om tanken är att spara vatten, finns det intelligenta duschmunstycken som med hjälp av sensorer kan rikta strålarna exakt till den plats där personen står, vilket gör att man slipper slösa med vatten. Likaså kan luftare installeras som sprider vattnet och minskar flödet genom att späda ut det med varm luft. Om man bygger in LED-belysning kan färgen på vattnet ändras i takt med vattentemperaturen eller så kan man byta efter behag när man ska ta sig ett bad.

Framsteg inom teknik och automation har också revolutionerat de så kallade intelligenta toaletterna, som även fungerar som bidéer och är programmerbara och justerbara. De har inbyggda självrengöringssystem och automatisk slutning som gör processen tystare. Hygien och komfort på toaletten kan garanteras genom uppvärmda sitsar och varmluftsspridare vid fötterna.

När det gäller möbler kan man välja speglar med pekskärm som innehåller musikanläggningar, radio, internet och till och med TV. Vissa är utformade för att göra livet lättare för äldre, eftersom de innehåller enkla program som är integrerade i själva spegeln och som påminner om allt från att borsta tänderna till att medicinerna ska tas.

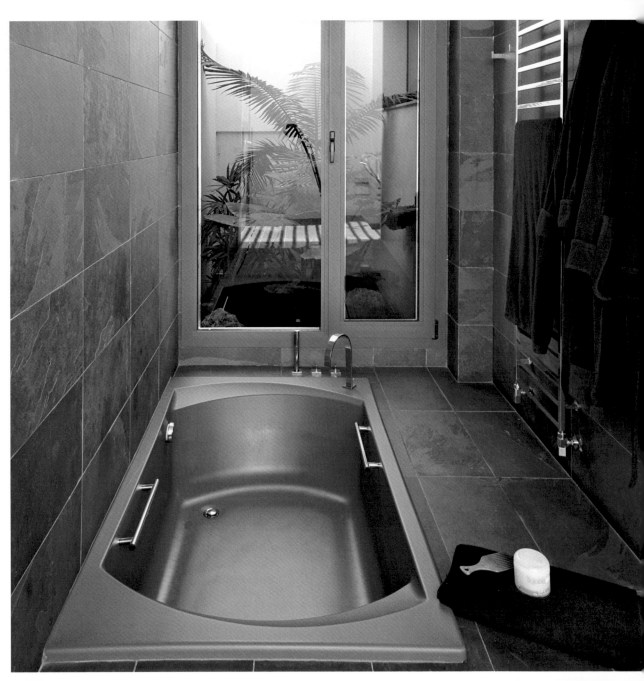

TIPS

© GRAFF

© GRAFF

Avoid unnecessary leaking and dripping. One drop per second turns into 30 litres of water per day (more than 10,000 litres per year).

Evita fugas y goteos innecesarios. Una gota por segundo se convierte en 30 litros de agua al día (más de 10.000 litros al año).

Évitez à tout prix les fuites et les robinets qui gouttent. Une goutte par seconde, c'est 30 litres d'eau par jour (et plus de 10 000 litres par an).

Evita fughe e gocciolamenti inutili. Una goccia al secondo equivale a 30 litri d'acqua al giorno (più di 10.000 litri l'anno).

Vermeiden Sie undichte Stellen und unnötige Feuchtigkeit. Ein Tropfen pro Sekunde sind 30 Liter pro Tag (mehr als 10.000 Liter pro Jahr).

Evite vazamentos e gotejamentos desnecessários. Uma gota por segundo transforma-se em 30 litros de água por dia (mais de 10 000 litros por ano).

Voorkom lekken en druppelende kranen. Een druppel per seconde is 30 liter water per dag en meer dan 10.000 liter per jaar.

Undvik onödiga läckage och dropp. En droppe i sekunden blir 30 liter vatten per dag (mer än 10 000 liter per år).

© GRAFF

© GRAFF

There are different models on the market offering automatic electronic systems with a sensor to save water.

Existen diferentes modelos en el mercado que ofrecen sistemas electrónicos automáticos que funcionan con un sensor para ahorrar agua.

Il existe aujourd'hui sur le marché différents modèles dotés de systèmes électroniques automatiques qui fonctionnent avec un capteur afin d'économiser l'eau.

Esistono vari modelli sul mercato che offrono sistemi elettronici automatici che funzionano con un sensore per risparmiare acqua.

Erhältlich sind viele automatisierte elektrische Systeme, die über einen Sensor verfügen und so Wasser sparen.

Existem no mercado diversos modelos com sistemas eletrônicos automáticos que funcionam com um sensor para poupar água.

Er zijn verschillende modellen in de handel die zijn voorzien van automatische elektronische systemen met waterbesparende sensoren.

Det finns olika modeller på marknaden med automatiserade elektroniska system som använder en sensor för att spara vatten.

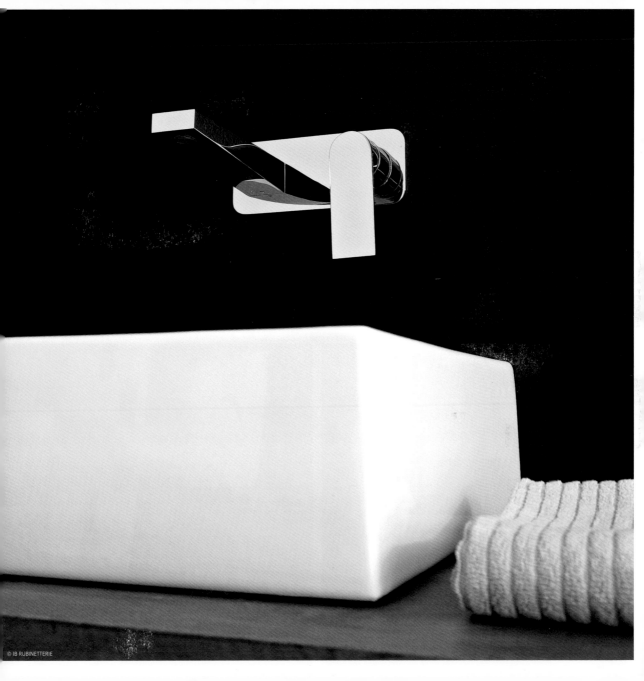

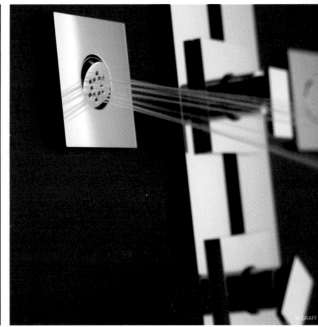

© TAU CERÁMICA

Water can be conserved in the shower by using flow switches, flow reducers, motion sensors or low-energy sprinklers.

Una forma de ahorrar agua en la ducha es mediante el uso de interruptores de caudal, perlizadores, sensores de movimiento o rociadores de bajo consumo.

L'une des façons d'économiser l'eau dans la douche est de s'équiper de limiteurs de débit, de mousseurs économiseurs d'eau, de détecteurs de mouvement ou de pommes de douche basse consommation.

Un modo per risparmiare l'acqua della doccia è tramite l'utilizzo di regolatori di portata, economizzatori d'acqua, sensori di movimento o soffioni a basso consumo.

Beim Duschen kann man durch einen unterbrochenen Wasserlauf, Perlator, Bewegungsmelder oder Duschkopf mit geringem Verbrauch Wasser sparen.

Uma forma de poupar água na ducha é através do uso de interruptores de fluxo, redutores, sensores de movimento ou pulverizadores de baixo consumo.

Een manier om douchewater te besparen zijn waterstroomonderbrekers, kraanmondstukken, bewegingssensoren en zuinige douchekoppen.

Ett sätt att spara vatten i duschen är att använda flödesvakter, luftare, rörelsesensorer eller vattensparande duschmunstycken.

© IB RUBINETTERIE

© IB RUBINETTERIE

Some more advanced shower stalls and bathtubs include chromotherapy systems for the enhancement of well-being during the shower.

Algunas cabinas de ducha o bañeras más avanzadas incorporan sistemas de cromoterapia para potenciar el bienestar durante la ducha.

Certaines cabines de douche ou de baignoire plus évoluées intègrent des systèmes de chromothérapie afin d'accroître les bienfaits de la douche.

Alcuni box doccia o vasche da bagno più all'avanguardia includono sistemi di cromoterapia per aumentare il benessere durante la doccia.

Es gibt Duschkabinen und fortschrittliche Badewannen, die Chromotherapiesysteme beinhalten und so das Wohlbefinden während des Duschens fördern.

Algumas cabines de ducha ou banheiras mais modernas incluem sistemas de cromoterapia, para maximizar o bemestar durante a ducha.

In sommige geavanceerde douchecabines of baden zijn kleurentherapiesystemen ingebouwd ter bevordering van het welbevinden tijdens het baden.

Vissa avancerade duschkabiner och badkar erbjuder färgterapi för att öka välbefinnandet under duschen.

© GRAFF

© GRAFF

125

While some companies offer different types of waterfall systems, it should be noted that a five-minute shower is sufficient for proper hygiene.

Aunque existen firmas que ofrecen diferentes sistemas de cascada de agua, hay que tener en cuenta que cinco minutos de ducha son suficientes para una correcta higiene.

Bien qu'il existe des entreprises qui proposent différents systèmes pour une arrivée d'eau en cascade, n'oubliez pas qu'une douche de cinq minutes suffit pour garder une bonne hygiène.

Anche se esistono marche che offrono diversi sistemi di cascata, bisogna tenere presente che cinque minuti di doccia sono sufficienti per una corretta igiene.

Auch wenn es Firmen gibt, die verschiedene Systeme für Duschköpfe anbieten, sollte man berücksichtigen, dass für die Hygiene fünf Minuten Duschen ausreichend sind.

Embora existam firmas que oferecem diferentes sistemas de cascata de água, temos que considerar que cinco minutos de ducha são suficientes para uma higiene correta.

Hoewel er ook watervalsystemen in de handel zijn, moeten we niet vergeten dat vijf minuten douchen voldoende is voor een goede hygiëne.

Även om olika företag erbjuder olika system med duschstrålar ska man komma ihåg att en fem minuters dusch är tillräcklig för god hygien.

© GRAFF

© DURAT

The higher the water temperature, the more energy is consumed: keeping it between 30 and 35 °C is sufficient for a comfortable shower.

Cuanto más alta sea la temperatura del agua, más energía consumiremos: mantenerla entre 30 y 35 °C es suficiente para una ducha confortable.

Plus la température de l'eau sera élevée, plus vous consommerez d'électricité : une eau entre 30 °C et 35 °C suffit pour que la douche soit agréable.

Più alta è la temperatura dell'acqua, più energia consumiamo: mantenerla tra i 30 e i 35 °C è sufficiente per una doccia gradevole.

Je höher die Wassertemperatur, desto mehr Energie verbrauchen wir: 30 bis 35 °C sind völlig ausreichend für eine angenehme Dusche.

Quanto mais elevada for a temperatura da água, mais energia consumimos: mantê-la entre 30 e 35°C é suficiente para uma ducha confortável.

Hoe hoger de watertemperatuur, des te meer energie we verbruiken. Voor een aangename douche is 30 tot 35 °C voldoende.

Ju högre vattentemperaturen är, desto mer energi förbrukar du: 30 till 35 °C räcker för en bekväm dusch.

MODERN-DAY LUXURY BATHROOMS

SALLES DE BAINS CONTEMPORAINES DE LUXE

MODERNE LUXUS-BÄDER

MODERNE LUXEBADKAMERS

BAÑOS CONTEMPORÁNEOS DE LUJO

BAGNI MODERNI DI LUSSO

CASAS DE BANHO CONTEMPORÂNEAS DE LUXO

MODERNA LYXIGA BADRUM

The most modern designs seek to combine luxury with comfort and functionality with attractiveness. The bathroom is no longer just a utilitarian space: it is now a place that provides pleasure. The innovations offered by new technology can transform this room into a true centre for well-being, not only with the inclusion of smart showers and mirrors but also with the use of high-quality materials.

With freestanding tubs and extra large saunas, the bathroom now resembles a salon. Long gone are the days when the bathroom was relegated to the background. Today, this space is reinventing itself with the help of architects and designers from around the world, so much so that it has come to be regarded as a main room in the house and is accessorized with features intended to maximize well-being. The objective is to convert the space into something that is more than a bathroom, into a private spa that can be used on a daily basis.

Bathtubs play a central role in the bathroom and have become a truly essential feature. The most luxurious are impressively large and either freestanding or built into the floor like miniature pools. The design takes into account even the smallest detail, including the location, which is often an exceptional place within the bathroom: in the middle of the floor, in front of a mirror, on a raised platform or even in an open-air location like on a porch or terrace. They can also include a hydro-massage system with a cascading stream of water.

As for materials, in addition to the classical elegance associated with stone (whether marble or limestone), ceramic tiling has also become quite popular for its easy maintenance and the possibilities for design and finishing that it offers. Mosaics, iridescent and metallic finishes and personalized designs transform the luxury bathroom into a space with a high level of distinction.

Les designs les plus modernes cherchent à créer des espaces combinant le luxe avec des environnements confortables, fonctionnels et attractifs. La salle de bains n'est plus un espace utile : c'est un lieu de plaisir. La technologie multiplie les innovations pour faire de cette pièce un véritable centre de bien-être, non seulement grâce à l'apport de douches et de miroirs intelligents mais aussi par l'utilisation de matériaux de grande qualité.

Baignoires isolées, saunas XXL... La salle de bains se décore aujourd'hui comme le salon. Cela fait bien longtemps que la salle de bains n'est plus reléguée au second plan. À l'heure actuelle, cet espace se réinvente grâce au talent d'architectes et de designers du monde entier. Et si bien que la salle de bains est considérée aujourd'hui comme une pièce principale et décorée au détail près pour assurer le bien-être maximal des utilisateurs. L'objectif premier consiste en effet à faire de cet espace quelque chose de plus qu'une simple salle de bains, à le transformer en un véritable spa privé qu'il est possible d'utiliser au quotidien.

Les baignoires passent au premier plan et s'imposent comme des éléments indispensables. Les tendances les plus luxueuses font la part belle aux baignoires de grandes dimensions, de plain-pied ou encastrées dans le sol comme s'il s'agissait d'une petite piscine. Le design d'une baignoire prend en compte jusqu'au moindre détail, à l'instar de son emplacement qui doit être un endroit privilégié : au centre de la pièce, placée dans un belvédère, en hauteur, voire à l'air libre sous un porche ou sur une terrasse. Et si votre baignoire dispose de surcroît d'un système d'hydromassage avec sortie d'eau en cascade, que demander de plus ?

Quant aux matériaux, à la pierre qui apporte une touche à la fois classique et élégante (qu'il s'agisse de marbre ou de calcaire) s'ajoutent les revêtements en céramique qui s'imposent avec force car ils sont faciles d'entretien et offrent de nombreuses possibilités de design et de finitions. Carrés de mosaïques, finitions irisées ou métallisées, designs personnalisés : ces éléments font de la salle de bains de luxe un espace des plus remarquables.

Modernes Design braucht Räume, um Luxus mit Komfort zu kombinieren und Funktionsfähigkeit anziehend zu machen. Das Bad ist nicht nur ein praktischer Ort: Es ist ein Ort des Vergnügens. Technische Innovationen ermöglichen es, dass man sich dort wirklich wohlfühlt. Hierzu dienen nicht nur intelligente Duschen und Spiegel, sondern auch qualitativ hochwertiges Material.

Freistehende Badewannen, XXL-Saunen...: Derzeit wird das Bad wie ein Wohnzimmer dekoriert. Die Zeiten, als das Bad nur eine untergeordnete Rolle spielte, sind vorbei. Inzwischen erfinden Architekten und Designer überall auf der Welt diesen Ort neu. Es ist ein wichtiger Aufenthaltsort und wird mit vielen Details dekoriert, um maximalen Komfort zu erlauben. Am Wichtigsten ist es, diesen Raum in etwas zu verwandeln, das über ein normales Bad hinausgeht, in einen „Spa", der täglich genutzt werden kann.

Das wichtigste Element sind Badewannen. Sie sind unumgänglich. Die neuesten Tendenzen hinsichtlich des Luxus beziehen sich auf die Größe, sie sind freistehend oder wie kleine Schwimmbäder in den Boden eingelassen. Ihr Design ist ausgeklügelt bis ins kleinste Detail, auch wenn sie sich in der Regel an einem privaten Ort befinden: im Zentrum, für den Betrachter sichtbar, erhöht oder sogar an der freien Luft in einem Porsche oder auf einer Terrasse. Und noch viel besser ist, dass sie sogar über ein Hydromassagesystem verfügen, bei dem ein Wasserstrahl ausströmt.

Zusätzlich zum klassischen und eleganten Stil, den Stein bietet, egal, ob es sich nun um Marmor oder Kalk handelt, wird nun auch immer mehr Keramik verwendet, da dieses Material leicht zu handhaben ist und eine Vielzahl von Möglichkeiten hinsichtlich Design und Verarbeitung bietet. Mosaike, schillernde Oberflächen, Metallverarbeitung und persönliches Design verwandeln das Bad in einen ganz eigenen Luxusort.

In de aller-modernste badkamers wordt gestreefd naar een optimale combinatie van comfort, functionaliteit en verleiding. De badkamer is niet meer een gewone gebruiksruimte, maar een ruimte die genot verschaft. Technologische innovaties maken het mogelijk om dit vertrek in een heus wellness-centrum in te richten, niet alleen met slimme douches en spiegels, maar ook met hoogwaardige materialen.

Vrijstaande badkuipen, XXL sauna's...: vandaag de dag wordt de badkamer ingericht als een woonvertrek. De jaren dat de badkamer op het tweede plan stond, liggen ver achter ons. Tegenwoordig wordt deze ruimte door architecten en ontwerpers opnieuw uitgevonden: hij wordt behandeld als een belangrijke ruimte en de inrichting is tot in detail gericht op behaaglijkheid. Voorop staat dat de ruimte meer moet zijn dan een simpele badkamer, namelijk een privé-waterbron die elke dag wordt gebruikt.

In dit verhaal speelt de badkuip een hoofdrol en is hij niet meer weg te denken. De meest luxueuze trend is een grote of vrijstaande badkuip, of in de vloer verzonken als een soort minizwembad. Over het ontwerp ervan is tot in detail nagedacht, net als over de plaats waar hij komt te staan, namelijk meestal op een bijzondere plek: in het midden, bij een raam, op een verhoging en zelfs in de open lucht op een veranda of terras. En als het even kan zit er nog een massagesysteem in met een watervalkraan.

Wat de gebruikte materialen betreft, wordt er naast het klassieke en chique natuursteen (zoals marmer of kalksteen) steeds meer keramiek toegepast omdat het weinig onderhoud vergt en diverse ontwerp- en afwerkingsmogelijkheden biedt. Mozaïeken, kleurrijke en metallic afwerkingen en persoonlijke ontwerpen maken de luxe badkamer tot een verfijnde ruimte.

Los diseños más modernos buscan espacios que combinen el lujo con la comodidad, la funcionalidad y la seducción. El baño ya no es un mero espacio de uso: se trata de un espacio de placer. La tecnología ofrece sus innovaciones para hacer de esta estancia un verdadero centro de bienestar, no solo con la incorporación de duchas y espejos inteligentes, sino también con el uso de materiales de alta calidad.

Bañeras aisladas, saunas XXL...: actualmente el baño se decora como el salón. Lejos quedan los años en los que el baño quedaba relegado a un segundo plano. Hoy, este espacio se reinventa de la mano de arquitectos y diseñadores de todo el mundo. Tanto, que se le da la categoría de estancia principal y se decora al detalle buscando el máximo bienestar. La prioridad consiste en convertirlo en algo más que un baño, en un *spa* privado que se pueda usar a diario.

Las bañeras toman protagonismo en la escena y se convierten en elementos imprescindibles. Las tendencias más lujosas apuestan por las grandes dimensiones, exentas o encastradas en el suelo como si se tratara de minipiscinas. Su diseño se cuida hasta el último detalle, igual que su ubicación, que suele estar en un sitio privilegiado: en el centro, asomada a un mirador, elevada o incluso al aire libre en un porche o en una terraza. Si, además, disponen de un sistema de hidromasaje con salida de agua en cascada, mucho mejor.

En cuanto a los materiales, además del clasicismo y la elegancia que aporta la piedra (ya sean mármoles o calizas), se imponen con fuerza los revestimientos cerámicos por su fácil mantenimiento y por las posibilidades de diseño y acabados que ofrecen. Mosaicos, acabados irisados, metalizados y diseños personalizados convierten el baño de lujo en un espacio con un alto grado de distinción.

I design più moderni ricercano spazi che mescolino il lusso a comfort, funzionalità e seduzione. Il bagno non è più un semplice spazio d'uso: si tratta di uno spazio di piacere. La tecnologia offre le sue innovazioni per rendere questa stanza un vero e proprio centro benessere, non solo con l'inclusione di docce e specchi intelligenti, ma anche con l'utilizzo di materiali di alta qualità.

Vasche da bagno isolate, saune XXL...: attualmente il bagno è arredato come il salotto. Sono lontani gli anni in cui il bagno era relegato a un secondo piano. Oggi, questo spazio è reinventato ad opera degli architetti e designer di tutto il mondo, al punto che gli viene attribuito lo status di camera principale ed è decorato nei minimi dettagli, alla ricerca del massimo benessere. La priorità sta nel farlo diventare qualcosa di più di un bagno, una *spa* privata che si possa utilizzare quotidianamente.

Le vasche da bagno assumono il ruolo di protagoniste sulla scena e si trasformano in elementi imprescindibili. Le tendenze di maggior lusso puntano sulle grandi dimensioni, libere o incassate nel pavimento come se si trattasse di minipiscine. Il loro design è curato fino all'ultimo dettaglio, così come la loro posizione, che normalmente è in un punto privilegiato: al centro, affacciata su una veranda, innalzata o addirittura all'aria aperta in un portico o su una terrazza. Se, in aggiunta, sono dotate di un sistema d'idromassaggio, con acqua a cascata, molto meglio.

Per quanto riguarda i materiali, oltre allo stile classico e all'eleganza che offre la pietra (sia i marmi che i calcari), s'impongono con forza i rivestimenti in ceramica grazie alla loro facile manutenzione e alle opportunità di design e finiture che offrono. Mosaici, finiture iridate, metallizzate e design personalizzati trasformano il bagno di lusso in uno spazio con un alto livello di distinzione.

Os *designs* mais modernos procuram espaços que combinem o luxo com o conforto, a funcionalidade e a sedução. O banho deixou de ser um mero espaço utilitário: trata-se de um espaço de prazer. A tecnologia faculta as suas inovações para fazer desta divisão um verdadeiro centro de bem-estar, não só através da introdução de duchas e espelhos inteligentes, mas também graças ao uso de materiais de alta qualidade.

Banheiras isoladas, saunas XXL... Atualmente, o banheiro é decorado com tanto cuidado quanto a sala. Longe vão os tempos em que ficava relegado para segundo plano. Hoje, este espaço é reinventado por arquitetos e *designers* de todo o mundo. Tanto, que se lhe atribui a categoria de divisão principal e se decora com detalhes, procurando o máximo bem-estar. A prioridade é fazer dele, mais do que um mero banheiro, um spa privado, que se pode usar diariamente.

As banheiras assumem aqui o protagonismo e transformam-se em elementos imprescindíveis. As tendências mais luxuosas apostam nas grandes dimensões, isoladas ou embutidas no chão, como se fossem minipiscinas. A sua concepção é cuidada até ao mais ínfimo pormenor, assim como a sua localização, habitualmente em lugar privilegiado: ao centro, junto de uma janela com vista, elevada ou até mesmo ao ar livre, sob um pórtico ou num terraço. Se, além disso, a banheira dispuser de um sistema de hidromassagem com saída da água em cascata, tanto melhor!

Quanto aos materiais, para além do classicismo e elegância da pedra (seja ela o mármore ou o calcário), impõem-se cada vez mais os revestimentos cerâmicos, devido à sua fácil manutenção e às possibilidades de *design* e de acabamentos que permitem. Mosaicos, acabamentos irisados e metalizados e *designs* personalizados fazem do banheiro de luxo um espaço com elevado grau de distinção.

Den mest moderna designen strävar efter rum som kombinerar lyx med bekvämlighet, funktionalitet och lockelse. Badrummet är inte längre bara funktionellt: det ska vara ett rum för njutning. Det finns tekniska innovationer som gör detta utrymme till ett riktigt hälsocenter, inte bara med smarta duschar och speglar, utan också med hjälp av högkvalitativa material.

Isolerade badkar, basturum av storlek XXL; för närvarande inreder man badrummen som vardagsrum. Det är länge sedan badrummen förpassades till bakgrunden. Idag håller utrymmet på att förvandlas i händerna på arkitekter och inredare över hela världen. Detta i så hög grad att rummet blivit ett av de viktigaste och inreds i detalj för största möjliga välbefinnande. Man prioriterar att förvandla det till något mer än bara ett badrum, gärna till ett privat *spa* som man kan använda dagligen.

Badkaren får huvudrollen och blir oumbärliga. De lyxigaste trenderna är stora dimensioner och fristående eller inbyggda i golvet som om de vore minibassänger. Designen är genomtänkt i minsta detalj och detsamma gäller placeringen, som ofta är på en privilegierad plats: i mitten, framför en spegel, på en förhöjning eller till och med i fria luften på en veranda eller terrass. Om det dessutom är ett bubbelbad med massageeffekt är det ännu bättre.

I materialen dominerar, utöver den klassiska och eleganta stenen (som marmor eller kalksten), keramiska ytor som kommer starkt tack vare det enkla underhållet och möjligheterna till design och olika ytbehandlingar som de erbjuder. Mosaik, regnbågsskimrande finish, metaller och personlig design gör lyxbadrummet högst unikt.

149

151

173

175

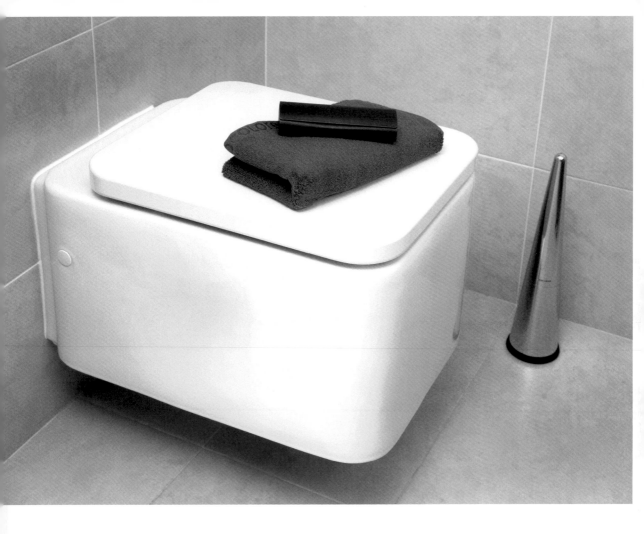

TIPS

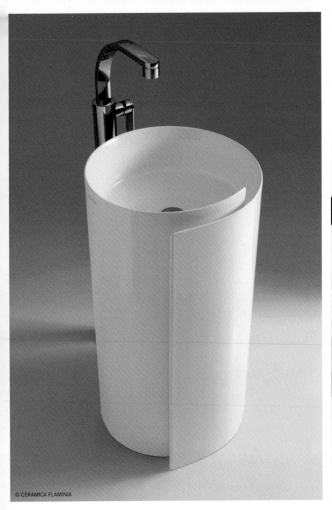

© CERAMICA FLAMINIA

© GRAFF

Select timeless features that stand out not only for their contemporary style but also for their comfort and practicality.

Selecciona piezas atemporales que destaquen no solo por su estilo contemporáneo, sino también por su confort y practicidad.

Choisissez des meubles intemporels qui se démarquent non seulement par leur style contemporain mais aussi par leur confort et leur côté pratique.

Scegli elementi senza tempo che si distinguano non solo per il loro stile contemporaneo, ma anche per il loro comfort e praticità.

Wählen Sie zeitgemäße Möbel, die nicht nur durch ihren modernen Stil, sondern auch durch ihren Komfort und ihren praktischen Nutzen hervorstechen.

Escolha peças intemporais que se destaquem não só pelo seu estilo contemporâneo, como também pelo seu conforto e funcionalidade.

Kies tijdloze meubels die niet alleen qua stijl opvallen, maar ook qua comfort en praktische bruikbaarheid.

Välj tidlösa möbler som inte bara sticker ut för att de är moderna, utan också är bekväma och praktiska.

199

© CERAMICA FLAMINIA

The contemporary bathroom is spacious, bright and simple. Choose bathroom fixtures with an optimal design, like wall-mounted toilets and bidets.

El baño contemporáneo es amplio, luminoso y sencillo. Elige un mobiliario sanitario con un diseño óptimo, como inodoros y bidés montados en la pared.

La salle de bains contemporaine est vaste, lumineuse et dépouillée. Choisissez un mobilier sanitaire au design optimal, comme par exemple des toilettes et des bidets suspendus au mur.

Il bagno contemporaneo è ampio, luminoso e semplice. Scegli dei sanitari con un ottimo design, come ad esempio water e bidet sospesi.

Derzeit ist das zeitgenössische Bad weitläufig, hell und schlicht. Wählen Sie Badmöbel mit optimalem Design, wie beispielsweise in die Wand eingelassene Toiletten und Bidets.

O banheiro contemporâneo é amplo, luminoso e simples. Escolha um mobiliário sanitário com um bom *design*, por exemplo, sanitário e bidés montados na parede.

Een hedendaagse badkamer is ruim, licht en eenvoudig. Kies voor sanitair met een optimaal ontwerp, zoals zwevende toiletten en bidets.

För tillfället är det moderna badrummet rymligt, ljust och enkelt. Välj sanitetsporslin med optimal design, som väggmonterade toaletter och bidéer.

© CERAMICA FLAMINIA

203

© CERAMICA FLAMINIA

Promote natural light with large windows. An oversized mirror is good for heightening the sense of spaciousness and brightness.

Favorece la iluminación natural con grandes aberturas. Un espejo de gran tamaño es un buen recurso para incrementar la sensación de amplitud y de luminosidad.

Privilégiez l'éclairage naturel avec de grandes ouvertures. Un miroir de grande taille est un bon moyen d'accroître la sensation de volume et de luminosité.

Favorisci l'illuminazione naturale con grandi aperture. Uno specchio di grandi dimensioni è un buono strumento per aumentare la sensazione di ampiezza e luminosità.

Heben Sie natürliches Licht durch große Öffnungen hervor. Ein großer Spiegel ist ideal, um den Eindruck von Weitläufigkeit und Helligkeit zu verstärken.

Favoreça a iluminação natural com grandes aberturas. Um espelho de grandes dimensões é um bom recurso para aumentar a sensação de amplitude e luminosidade.

Zorg voor zo veel mogelijk daglicht. Een grote spiegel is een uitstekend hulpmiddel om het gevoel van ruimtelijkheid en licht te versterken.

Släpp in dagsljuset genom stora öppningar. En stor spegel är en bra metod för att öka känslan av rymd och ljus.

© APARIC

© CERAMICA FLAMINI

If you have an urban apartment, choose a hand-held shower that fuses art, technology and design. Many of them provide an experience that exceeds expectations.

Si tu apartamento es urbano escoge teleduchas que fusionen arte, tecnología y diseño. Muchas de ellas ofrecen una experiencia que sobrepasa las expectativas.

Si votre appartement est de style urbain, optez pour une pomme de douche mêlant l'art, la technologie et le design. Nombre de ces modèles de douchettes vous offriront une expérience au-delà de toutes vos attentes.

Se il tuo appartamento è urbano, scegli telefoni da doccia che combinino arte, tecnologia e design. Molti di questi offrono un'esperienza che supera le attese.

Für ein urbanes Apartment könnten Sie eine Luxusdusche wählen, die Kunst, Technologie und Design vereint. Viele dieser Duschen bieten Erfahrungen, die alle Erwartungen übertreffen.

Se o seu apartamento for urbano, escolha chuveiros de mão em que mesclem arte, tecnologia e *design*. Muitos deles proporcionam uma experiência que ultrapassa todas as expectativas.

In een stadsappartement is een douchekop waarin kunst, technologie en design samenkomen op zijn plaats. Vaak bieden ze een ervaring die alle verwachtingen overtreft.

Om din lägenhet är urbant inredd finns det duschmunstycken som sammanför konst, teknik och design. Många ger en upplevelse som överträffar förväntningarna.

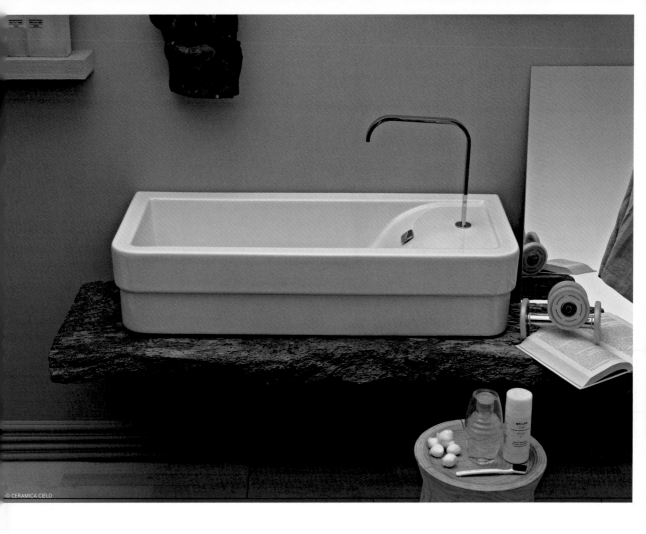

213

Bathtubs in these types of spaces are characterized by their soft lines. Choose from among a variety of dimensions and features and pick the product that best meets your needs.

Las bañeras de este tipo de espacios se caracterizan por sus líneas suaves. Elige entre varias medidas y características y opta por el producto que más se adecue a tus requerimientos.

Les baignoires de ce type d'espaces se caractérisent par leurs lignes fluides. Vous disposez d'un large choix en termes de dimensions et d'accessoires et vous pouvez donc choisir le produit qui correspond le mieux à vos exigences.

Le vasche da bagno di questo tipo di spazi sono caratterizzate dalle loro linee morbide. Scegli fra varie misure e caratteristiche e preferisci il prodotto che meglio si adatta alle tue esigenze.

Badewannen dieser Art bestechen durch ihre sanften Linien. Wählen Sie zwischen vielen Möglichkeiten und Eigenschaften und entscheiden Sie sich für das Modell, das am ehesten Ihren Bedürfnissen entspricht.

As banheiras deste tipo de espaço caracterizam-se pelas suas linhas suaves. Escolha entre várias medidas e características e opte pelo produto que melhor se adeque às suas necessidades.

Badkuipen in dit soort ruimtes worden gekenmerkt door zachte lijnen. Vergelijk verschillende maten en eigenschappen en kies het product dat het meest aan uw wensen voldoet.

Badkar i den här typen av rum kännetecknas av mjuka linjer. Välj mellan olika storlekar och funktioner och ta den produkt som bäst passar dina behov.

The functionality and durability of the surfaces are crucial for achieving a space that is conducive to relaxation and well-being.

La funcionalidad y la durabilidad de los acabados son imprescindibles para conseguir un espacio que invite a la relajación y el bienestar.

Il est fondamental d'avoir des finitions fonctionnelles et durables pour obtenir un espace invitant à la relaxation et au bien-être.

La funzionalità e la durata delle finiture sono imprescindibili per ottenere uno spazio che inviti al relax e al benessere.

Funktionalität und Langlebigkeit der Verarbeitung sind unerlässlich für einen Ort; der zum Entspannen und Wohlfühlen einlädt.

A funcionalidade e durabilidade dos acabamentos são imprescindíveis para conseguir um espaço que convide ao relaxamento e ao bemestar.

Functionaliteit en duurzaamheid zijn medebepalend voor een ruimte waarin u zich goed voelt en kunt ontspannen.

Funktionell och hållbar finish är avgörande för att åstadkomma ett rum som inbjuder till avkoppling och välbefinnande.

223

WORKADAY BATHROOMS

SALLES DE BAINS CLASSIQUES

HERKÖMMLICHE BÄDER

ALLEDAAGSE BADKAMERS

BAÑOS HABITUALES

BAGNI DI TUTTI I GIORNI

BANHEIROS TRIVIAIS

BADRUM FÖR VARDAGSBRUK

Everything is easy with a lot of space, but what happens when you only have a small area for a bathroom? Good initial planning is essential for getting the most out of the design and layout of the bathroom while also making it a pleasant space.

One of the basic premises is to organize the elements that make up the bathroom (toilet, sink, shower) in an orderly manner which makes it possible to maximize the space, however small it may be, while enabling easy movement and allowing comfortable and functional access to all of its features. The largest elements like the shower or bathtub will be found in the back of the room. Likewise, to separate the shower area from the rest of the bathroom, transparent glass panels or a curtain can be used, rather than frosted or treated glass. This provides a sense of openness and allows the full dimensions of the bathroom to be seen.

The issue of where to store objects in the bathroom can often be problematic. There are many low cabinets with useful drawers available on the market. If there is not enough space for a cabinet, shelves can be used instead. This allows all accessories to be kept in sight and minimizes the time required to find them. For the storage of towels, which take up a great deal of space, the area under the sink can be used for a small cabinet. Towel rails can be purchased at low cost, enabling towels to be kept parallel to the wall and thus saving space.

As for wall surfaces, alternative materials are popular, with waterproof paint in colours ranging from yellow to white for greater luminosity and spaciousness.

At the same time, lighting must be sufficient for performing all necessary tasks. Options include light bulbs built into a false ceiling or halogen lights along the frame of the mirror.

Tout est facile quand on dispose de beaucoup de place mais comment faire pour installer une salle de bains dans un espace réduit ? Il est indispensable de déterminer dès le début un agencement optimal afin de tirer profit au maximum des proportions et de l'aménagement de la salle de bains sans pour autant renoncer à en faire un espace agréable.

L'une des étapes fondamentales consiste à organiser les éléments qui composent la salle de bains (toilettes, lavabo, douche) et à les ordonner de façon à maximiser l'espace, aussi petit soit-il. Cela permet de s'assurer de circuler facilement dans la pièce et surtout que tous les meubles sont facilement d'accès et fonctionnels. Les éléments de volume important comme la douche ou la baignoire doivent être placés au fond de la pièce. En outre, pour séparer la zone de douche du reste de la pièce, il est recommandé d'utiliser des parois en verre transparent plutôt que du verre dépoli, traité ou encore un simple rideau. Cela permet d'exploiter les effets de transparence et de percevoir les dimensions de la pièce dans leur intégralité.

Le problème le plus fréquent reste le rangement des objets divers se trouvant dans une salle de bains. Il existe sur le marché un grand nombre d'armoires basses dotées de tiroirs bien utiles. Si vous ne disposez pas d'un espace suffisant pour y placer une armoire, vous pouvez opter pour des étagères. Ainsi, tous vos accessoires seront bien en vue et vous ne perdrez plus votre temps à les chercher. Pour ranger les serviettes qui prennent toujours beaucoup de place, il est possible d'exploiter la partie inférieure du lavabo et d'y placer une petite armoire. Il est également possible d'acquérir à bas prix des radiateurs qui font aussi office de porte-serviettes et qui permettent de garder les serviettes parallèles au mur, ce qui constitue une belle économie de l'espace.

Quant aux revêtements, il est recommandé d'utiliser des matériaux alternatifs et d'opter pour des peintures hydrofuges avec des gammes de couleurs allant du jaune au blanc pour donner plus de luminosité et d'ampleur à la pièce.

Par ailleurs, l'éclairage doit être adapté pour vous permettre de prendre agréablement soin de vous au quotidien. Vous pouvez choisir des spots encastrés dans un faux plafond ou des lampes halogènes fixées au cadre du miroir.

Wenn einem viel Platz zur Verfügung steht, ist alles einfach. Aber was macht man, wenn man nur wenig Platz für ein Bad zur Verfügung hat? Es gilt, eine geeignete Grundfläche für das bestmögliche Design und die beste Platznutzung zu finden und ihm dennoch einen angenehmen Charakter zu verleihen.

Wichtig ist es, die Elemente des Bades (Toilette, Waschbecken, Dusche) so anzuordnen, dass möglich viel Platz geschaffen wird, egal, wie klein der Raum ist. Außerdem müssen zurückzulegende Wege vereinfacht werden, also die Elemente auf eine geeignete und funktionsdienliche Weise angeordnet werden. Die großen Komponenten wie Dusche oder Badewanne werden an der Vorderseite aufgestellt. Um den Bereich der Dusche vom restlichen Bad abzutrennen, können Vorhänge oder durchsichtige Glaswände, anstatt mattierte oder beschichtete, eingezogen werden. So kann man die Transparenz genießen und es stehen die gesamten Dimensionen des Bades zur Verfügung.

Oft stellt sich das Problem, wo man die Badeutensilien aufbewahren kann. Es gibt viele kleine Schränke mit nützlichen Schubladen. Wenn es keinen Platz für einen Schrank gibt, kann dieser auch durch Regale ersetzt werden. So sehen Sie all Ihr Zubehör und brauchen weniger Zeit, es zu finden. Das Unterbringen der Handtücher braucht viel Platz. Hierfür kann ein Schrank unter dem Waschbecken verwendet werden. Es gibt preisgünstige Handtuchheizer. Diese ermöglichen es, die Handtücher platzsparend an der Wand anzubringen.

Für die Verkleidung werden alternative Materialien verwendet. Diese werden durch wasserfeste Bilder verschönert. Die Farbpalette reicht hier von gelb bis weiß. Dies erzeugt mehr Helligkeit und Raum.

Es braucht ausreichend Licht, um alle Tätigkeiten ausführen zu können. Man kann sich für eingebaute Lampen in Zwischendecken oder Halogenleuchten im Spiegelrand entscheiden.

Als er vierkante meters te over zijn is alles gemakkelijk, maar wat als er voor de badkamer maar weinig ruimte beschikbaar is? Ook in dat geval kan met een goed doordacht ontwerp en een uitgekiende inrichting van de badkamer een aangename ruimte worden gecreëerd.

Een van de uitgangspunten is de onderdelen van de badkamer (toilet, wastafel, douche) zo te organiseren dat de ruimte, hoe klein ook, maximaal wordt benut en dat tegelijkertijd alle functionele elementen gemakkelijk bereikbaar zijn zonder allerlei ingewikkelde manoeuvres te hoeven uitvoeren. De grootste elementen zoals de douche of het bad komen achterin. Daarnaast wordt het douchegedeelte met een doorzichtig gordijn of een scherm van transparant glas van de rest afgescheiden. Zo draagt transparantie ertoe bij dat de afmetingen van de ruimte visueel niet worden ingeperkt.

Meer dan eens is opbergruimte in de badkamer een probleem. Er zijn verschillende lage kasten met handige laden op de markt. Als er geen ruimte voor een kast is, kunnen er schappen worden opgehangen. Zo liggen alle benodigdheden in het zicht en verspilt u niet onnodig tijd met zoeken. Handdoeken, die altijd veel ruimte in beslag nemen, kunt u opbergen in een klein kastje onder de wastafel. Ook bestaan er betaalbare handdoekradiatoren die tegen de wand worden geplaatst, waarmee u veel ruimte bespaart.

Voor de afwerking van muren en vloeren worden alternatieve materialen gebruikt en waterafstotende verf in een kleurenspectrum van geel tot wit voor meer licht en een ruimtelijk effect.

Ook de verlichting moet goed zijn zodat alle badkamerbezigheden goed kunnen worden uitgevoerd. U kunt kiezen voor spotjes in een verlaagd plafond of halogeenverlichting rond de spiegel.

Todo es fácil cuando sobran metros, pero ¿qué pasa cuando solo se dispone de un espacio pequeño destinado al cuarto de baño? Hace falta un buen planteamiento inicial para sacar el máximo partido del diseño y la distribución del baño sin renunciar a un espacio agradable.

Una de las premisas básicas es organizar los elementos que componen el baño (inodoro, lavabo, ducha) de una forma ordenada que permita maximizar el espacio, por pequeño que sea, a la vez que simplifique los recorridos y permita acceder a todas las piezas de forma cómoda y funcional. Los elementos con mayor volumen, como la ducha o la bañera, se colocarán al fondo del plano. Asimismo, para separar la zona de la ducha del resto del baño, se optará por mamparas de vidrio transparente, en vez de esmerilado o tratado, o por una cortina. De esa forma, se aprovechan las transparencias y se perciben las dimensiones del cuarto por completo.

Muchas veces, el problema radica en dónde guardar los objetos del cuarto de baño. Existen en el mercado diferentes armarios bajos con útiles cajones. Si no hay espacio para colocar un armario, se puede sustituir por unas estanterías. Así todos los accesorios estarán a la vista y perderás menos tiempo a la hora de localizarlos. Para almacenar las toallas que ocupan mucho espacio se puede aprovechar la parte inferior del lavamanos para colocar un pequeño armario. Existen toalleros-radiadores a un precio económico que permiten tener las toallas paralelas a la pared, con el consecuente ahorro de espacio.

En cuanto a los revestimientos, se imponen los materiales alternativos y se opta por pinturas impermeables con gamas de color que van del amarillo al blanco para conseguir una mayor luminosidad y amplitud.

Por otro lado, la iluminación debe ser adecuada para poder realizar todas las tareas necesarias. Se puede optar por focos empotrados en falso techo o por luces halógenas en el marco del espejo.

Tutto è più semplice quando i metri sono tanti, ma cosa succede quando si ha a disposizione solo un piccolo spazio destinato al bagno? È necessario un buon progetto iniziale per ottenere il massimo dal design e la distribuzione del bagno, senza rinunciare ad uno spazio piacevole.

Una delle premesse fondamentali è organizzare gli elementi che compongono il bagno (water, lavandino, doccia) in un modo ordinato che consenta l'ottimizzazione dello spazio, per quanto piccolo, e allo stesso tempo faciliti i percorsi e permetta di accedere comodamente e in modo funzionale a tutte le parti. Gli elementi con maggiore volume come la doccia o la vasca da bagno saranno disposti sul fondo della pianta. Allo stesso modo, per separare la zona doccia dal resto del bagno, si sceglieranno paraventi di vetro trasparente, invece che smerigliato o trattato, o una tenda. Così facendo, si sfruttano le trasparenze e si percepiscono le dimensioni della stanza nell'insieme.

In molti casi, il problema consiste nel dove sistemare gli oggetti della stanza da bagno. Esistono sul mercato svariati armadi bassi con utili cassetti. Se non c'è spazio per disporre un armadio, può essere sostituito con degli scaffali. In questo modo, tutti gli accessori saranno in vista e perderete meno tempo per trovarli. Per riporre gli asciugamani che occupano molto spazio, si può sfruttare la parte inferiore del lavabo per sistemare un piccolo armadio. Esistono caloriferi-scaldaasciugamani ad un prezzo economico, che consentono di tenere gli asciugamani paralleli alla parete, con il conseguente risparmio di spazio.

Per quanto riguarda i rivestimenti, s'impongono i materiali alternativi e si scelgono vernici impermeabili con gamme di colore che vanno dal giallo al bianco per ottenere una maggiore luminosità e ampiezza.

D'altra parte, l'illuminazione deve essere adatta per svolgere tutte le attività necessarie. È possibile scegliere faretti da incasso in soffitto in cartongesso o luci alogene nella cornice dello specchio.

Tudo é fácil quando nos sobram metros, mas, o que é que acontece quando apenas dispomos de um espaço reduzido para o banheiro? É muito importante um bom planejamento inicial para tirar o máximo partido do *design* e da distribuição do espaço do banheiro, sem renunciar ao seu aspeto agradável.

Uma das premissas básicas é organizar os elementos que constituem o banheiro (sanitário, pia, ducha) de uma forma ordenada, que permita maximizar o espaço, por pequeno que seja, e ao mesmo tempo simplifique os percursos e permita aceder a todos os elementos de forma confortável e funcional. Os elementos de maior volume, como a ducha o a banheira, devem ser colocados ao fundo do plano. Do mesmo modo, para separar a zona da ducha do resto do banheiro, deve-se optar por resguardos de vidro transparente, em vez de esmerilhado ou tratado, ou por uma cortina. Deste modo, aproveitam-se as transparências e a divisão é percebida nas suas dimensões totais.

Muitas vezes, o problema está em onde guardar os objetos do banheiro. Existem no mercado diversos modelos de armários baixos com gavetas providenciais. Se não houver espaço para colocar um armário, este pode ser substituído por prateleiras. Assim, todos os acessórios ficam à vista e não se perde tempo a sua procura. Para guardar as toalhas, que ocupam muito espaço, pode-se aproveitar a parte de baixo do lavatório para colocar um pequeno armário. Existem também toalheiros-radiadores a um preço económico, que permitem manter as toalhas paralelas à parede, com a consequente poupança de espaço.

Em relação aos revestimentos, impõem-se os materiais alternativos e opta-se por uma pintura com tinta impermeável com gamas de cor que vão do amarelo ao branco, para conseguir uma maior luminosidade e amplitude.

Por outro lado, a iluminação deve ser adequada para poder realizar todas as tarefas necessárias. Pode-se optar por focos embutidos num teto falso ou por lâmpadas de halógenas na moldura do espelho.

Det är hur lätt som helst när man har gott om utrymme, men vad händer när det bara finns ett litet utrymme för badrummet? Det är viktigt med en bra ursprungsstrategi för att få ut så mycket som möjligt av designen och badrumslayouten och ändå få det till en behaglig plats.

En av de grundläggande förutsättningarna är att organisera de nödvändiga inslagen i badrummet (toalett, handfat, dusch) på ett sätt som maximerar utrymmet, hur litet det än är, samtidigt som man förenklar linjerna och ger bekvämt och smidigt tillträde till alla delar. De delar som tar störst plats, som dusch eller badkar, placeras längst bort. Dessutom kan man välja genomskinliga glasskärmar istället för kakelvägg eller duschdraperi för att avskärma duschen från resten av rummet. Man drar på så sätt nytta av genomskinligheten och upplever hela rummet.

Ofta är problemet var man ska förvara alla prylar som behövs i badrummet. Det finns olika typer av skåp att marknaden som kan vara till stor hjälp. Om det inte finns utrymme för ett skåp kan man istället sätta upp några hyllor. Då har man alla prylar inom synhåll och slipper lägga ned tid på att leta efter dem. För att förvara alla handdukar som tar upp plats kan man utnyttja utrymmet under handfatet för ett litet skåp. Det finns handdukstorkar till ett överkomligt pris som gör att man kan förvara handdukarna parallellt med väggen, vilket sparar utrymme.

Materialmässigt använder man alternativa beläggningar och väljer ofta vattentåliga färger i nyanser som varierar från gult till vitt för att ge ökad ljusstyrka och rymlighet.

Dessutom måste belysningen vara tillräcklig för alla vardagsuppgifter. Man kan sätta in spotlights i innertaket eller halogenlampor i spegeln.

257

TIPS

© DURAT

© DURAT

In smaller bathrooms, a good option is to hang furniture with ample interior space.

En los baños estrechos o de reducidas dimensiones, una buena opción es colocar muebles suspendidos con una gran capacidad interior.

Dans les salles de bains étroites ou de dimensions réduites, il est recommandé d'installer des meubles suspendus dotés d'une grande capacité de stockage.

Nei bagni stretti o di dimensioni ridotte, una buona scelta è quella di collocare mobili sospesi dotati di una grande capacità interna.

Für enge oder begrenzte Bäder empfehlen sich Möbel mit viel Stauraum.

Nos banheiros estreitos ou de dimensões reduzidas, uma boa opção é colocar móveis suspensos de grande capacidade interior.

In smalle of kleine badkamers zijn hangmeubelen met veel binnenruimte een goede optie.

I smala eller små badrum är det ett bra alternativ att välja vägghängda möbler med stor kapacitet för förvaring.

© DURAT

277

Modular furniture is always a good choice, as it enables you to adapt the pieces to the space available.

El mobiliario modular es siempre una buena elección ya que permite adaptar las piezas al espacio disponible.

Le mobilier modulable est toujours un bon choix car il vous permet d'adapter les meubles à l'espace disponible.

I mobili modulari sono sempre una buona scelta perché permettono di adattare gli elementi allo spazio disponibile.

Modulare Möbel sind hier immer ideal, da man sie an den verfügbaren Platz anpassen kann.

O mobiliário modular é sempre uma boa escolha, pois permite adaptar as peças ao espaço disponível.

Modulair meubilair is altijd een goede keuze omdat het zich laat aanpassen aan de beschikbare ruimte.

Modulmöbler är alltid ett bra val eftersom man kan anpassa dem efter utrymmet.

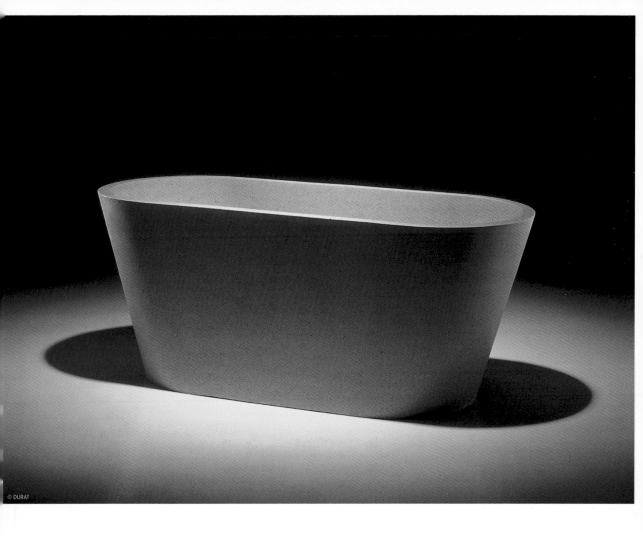

© DURAT

© DURAT

A muted colour palette will foster calmness and serenity, though an occasional note of colour can break the monotony and create a more striking style.

Una paleta acotada de colores aportará calma y serenidad, aunque una nota de color, en ocasiones, puede romper con la sobriedad y aportar un estilo más impactante.

Une palette limitée de couleurs vous permet d'instaurer une ambiance calme et sereine, quoiqu'une touche de couleurs ici et là permet de rompre la sobriété et de donner un style plus marquant.

Una gamma limitata di colori apporterà calma e serenità, anche se un tocco di colore, a volte, può spezzare la sobrietà e conferire uno stile di maggiore impatto.

Eine begrenzte Farbauswahl bringt Ruhe und Ausgeglichenheit, wohingegen zu viel Farbe manchmal übertrieben wirkt und zu einem Stilbruch führt.

Uma paleta limitada de cores confere calma e serenidade, embora uma nota de cor possa, por vezes, romper com a sobriedade e conseguir um estilo com maior impacto.

Een beperkt kleurenpalet zorgt voor serene rust, maar soms kan een kleuraccent ook de soberheid doorbreken en een statement vormen.

En enhetlig färgpalett ger lugn och ro, medan några färgklickar kan bryta av och ge ett starkare intryck.

283

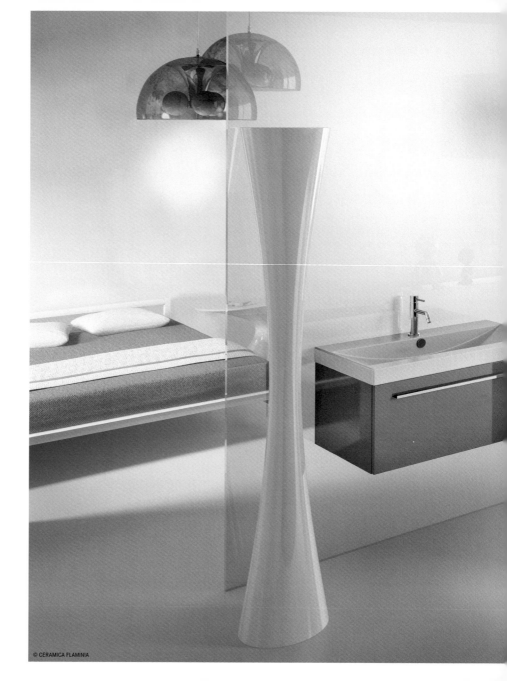

© CERAMICA FLAMINIA

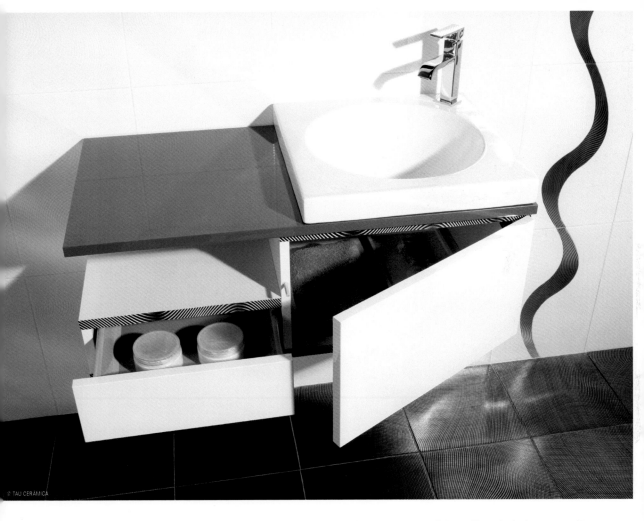

© TAU CERÀMICA

Select functional and compact pieces without sacrificing originality. There are units available that perform multiple functions and help to save space.

Elige piezas funcionales y compactas sin renunciar a la originalidad. Hay módulos que integran varias funciones y permiten economizar espacio.

Choisissez des meubles fonctionnels et compacts sans pour autant renoncer à l'originalité. Il existe des modules qui intègrent de multiples fonctions et permettent d'économiser de l'espace.

Scegli elementi funzionali e compatti senza rinunciare all'originalità. Ci sono moduli che racchiudono varie funzioni e consentono di economizzare spazio.

Wählen Sie funktionelle und kompakte Möbel ohne dabei die Originalität außer Acht zu lassen. Es gibt Multifunktionsmodelle, mit denen sich Platz sparen lässt.

Escolha peças funcionais e compactas sem renunciar à originalidade. Há módulos que integram várias funções e permitem economizar espaço.

Kies voor functionele en compacte stukken zonder van originaliteit af te zien. Er zijn ook ruimtebesparende multifunctionele modules.

Välj funktionell och kompakt inredning, utan att ge avkall på originaliteten. Det finns moduler som integrerar olika funktioner och sparar på utrymmet.

293

© CERAMICA CIELO

297

You will find a full range of modular bathroom furniture on the market, with different finishes, styles, sizes and prices.

En el mercado encontrarás una completa gama de muebles de baño modulares, con diferentes acabados y de diferentes estilos, medidas y precios.

Sur le marché, vous trouverez une vaste gamme de meubles de bains modulables, aux finitions, aux styles, aux dimensions et aux prix multiples.

Sul mercato troverai una gamma completa di mobili da bagno modulari, con finiture differenti e di vari stili, dimensioni e prezzi.

Auf dem Markt ist eine Vielzahl dieser Badmodule mit unterschiedlicher Verarbeitung und Maßen und zu unterschiedlichen Preisen erhältlich.

Poderá encontrar no mercado uma completa gama de móveis de banheiro modulares, com diferentes acabamentos e de diferentes estilos, medidas e preços.

Er is een breed assortiment aan modulaire badkamermeubelen in de handel met verschillende afwerkingen en in verschillende stijlen, maten en prijzen.

På marknaden hittar du ett komplett sortiment av modulära badrumsmöbler med olika ytbehandling och i olika stil, storlek och pris.

BARE-ESSENTIAL BATHROOMS

SALLES DE BAINS ESSENTIELLES

ESSENZIELLE BÄDER

BASALE BADKAMERS

BAÑOS ESENCIALES

BAGNI ESSENZIALI

BANHEIROS MINIMALISTAS

ENKLA BADRUM

Minimalism is one of the leading styles in bathroom design. In minimalist bathrooms, less is more, except when it comes to light and space. Minimalist bathrooms are often made using white ceramic (for furniture) combined with glass, marble and steel for the accessories and other elements like the floor and partitions. The lines are clean and without ornamentation.

This style is more adapted to the bathrooms of individuals and couples, as spaces that are cluttered with objects, as in the case of family bathrooms, conflict with the overall aesthetic. Towels and other bath items are stored in built-in cabinets and drawers, so as not to interfere with the angular symmetry of the room.

Today, it is possible for bathrooms to be designed using an infinite number of materials. While marble remains the most popular material, especially for elegant bathrooms, with stone and glass having gained ground, it is hard to imagine that the functionality of ceramic tubs and sinks will ever be surpassed.

The minimalist style also leads us to open and monochromatic spaces, though some feature a note of colour to add a touch of sophistication. In addition to white, we may also encounter sharp colours and timeless classics like wood and neutral tones.

With regard to furniture, preference is given to straight lines and geometric shapes. The dimensions of the bathroom are often small. The minimalist style provides added spaciousness, as it requires things to be kept in order. All specialized companies currently have models matching this functional and stripped-down style for accessories.

Le minimalisme figure parmi les styles les plus populaires pour le design des salles de bains. Dans les salles de bains minimalistes, le concept *less is more* s'applique, sauf quand il s'agit de ces deux éléments principaux : la lumière et l'espace. En règle générale, les salles de bains minimalistes sont composées d'éléments en céramique blanche (pour le mobilier) combinés à des accessoires en verre, en marbre et en acier ainsi qu'à d'autres composants tels que le sol et les pare-douches. Les lignes sont simples et épurées.

Ce style est particulièrement adapté aux salles de bains de personnes célibataires ou en couple dans la mesure où les espaces surchargés d'objets, associés aux salles de bains familiales, vont à l'encontre de l'esthétique prédominante. Les serviettes et autres éléments de la salle de bains sont conservés dans des armoires et des tiroirs encastrés afin qu'ils n'interfèrent pas avec la symétrie à angles droits de la pièce.

De nos jours, le design d'une salle de bains peut reposer sur une infinité de matériaux. En dépit du fait que le marbre reste le matériau par excellence, surtout dans les salles de bains élégantes, et bien que la pierre et le verre gagnent en popularité, il reste difficile d'imaginer qu'ils surpassent un jour les baignoires et les lavabos en céramique en termes de fonctionnalité.

Le style minimaliste mène également à des espaces diaphanes et monochromes, bien que parfois, une note de couleur soit ajoutée afin d'apporter une touche sophistiquée. En plus du blanc, ces espaces peuvent comporter des couleurs acides et d'éternels classiques tels que le bois et les tons neutres.

En matière de mobilier, il est de mise d'opter pour des lignes droites et des meubles aux formes géométriques. En règle générale, les dimensions de la salle de bains sont petites. Grâce au style minimaliste, l'espace gagne en ampleur car le minimalisme vous oblige à garder chaque chose à sa place. À l'heure actuelle, toutes les entreprises spécialisées proposent des modèles en adéquation avec ce style fonctionnel et dépouillé d'accessoires.

Minimalismus ist ein in Bädern vorherrschender Stil. In minimalistischen Bädern ist weniger mehr, außer es handelt sich um die Grundelemente: Licht und Raum. In der Regel sind diese minimalistischen Bäder aus weißem Keramik (bei den Möbeln), kombiniert mit Glas, Marmor und Stahl für die Accessoires und anderen Elementen wie Boden und Wänden. Die Linien sind gerade und ohne Verzierungen.

Dieser Stil wird vor allem für die Bäder von Singles und Paaren verwendet, da mit Objekten überhäufte Orte, wie sie für Familienbäder typisch sind, der vorherrschenden Ästhetik widersprechen. Die Handtücher werden in Schränken und eingebauten Boxen aufbewahrt, um nicht im Konflikt zu den rechten Winkeln des Raumes zu stehen.

Eigentlich können diese Bäder heutzutage mit unendlich vielen Materialien eingerichtet werden. Einmal ganz davon abgesehen, dass Marmor immer noch das vorherrschende Material vor allem für elegante Bäder ist, und obwohl Stein und Glas immer beliebter werden, fällt es schwer sich vorzustellen, dass sie irgendwann die Funktionsfähigkeit von Badewannen und Waschbecken aus Keramik übertreffen.

Der minimalistische Stil führt uns auch hin zu durchscheinenden und einfarbigen Orten, auch wenn teilweise ein Hauch Farbe miteinfließt, um dem Ganzen einen Anstrich von Komplexität zu verpassen. Zusätzlich zu Weiß findet man auch knallige Farben und die ewigen Klassiker wie Holzfarben und neutrale Töne.

Bezüglich des Mobiliars finden sich rechte Winkel und Möbel in geometrischen Formen. Normalerweise sind die Dimensionen des Badezimmers reduziert. Der minimalistische Stil erlaubt ein Plus an Weitläufigkeit, da er dazu zwingt, seine Sachen in Ordnung zu halten. Aktuell setzen alle Fachfirmen auf Modelle, die diesen funktionellen Stil und den Verzicht auf Accessoires berücksichtigen.

Het minimalisme is een van de stijlen die bij het ontwerp van badkamers de boventoon voeren. In een minimalistische badkamer geldt "minder is meer", behalve wat de basiselementen licht en ruimte betreft. Het meubilair in een minimalistische badkamer is meestal van wit keramiek, gecombineerd met glas, marmer, stalen accessoires en andere materialen voor de vloer en douchechermen. De lijnvoering is zuiver en strak.

Deze stijl is vooral geschikt voor alleenstaanden en stellen, omdat allerlei rondslingerende spullen, zoals vaak in gezinsbadkamers het geval is, niet goed samengaan met minimalistische esthetiek. Handdoeken en andere toiletartikelen worden opgeborgen in kasten en inbouwladen zodat de symmetrie van de rechte hoeken niet wordt verstoord.

Tegenwoordig zijn badkamerontwerpen in allerlei materialen mogelijk. Marmer is nog altijd nummer één, met name bij chique badkamers, en hoewel natuursteen en glas terrein hebben gewonnen, is het moeilijk voor te stellen dat deze op een dag de functionaliteit van baden en wastafels van keramiek gaan overtreffen.

Het minimalisme heeft ons ook heldere en eenkleurige ruimtes gebracht, hoewel er soms voor enig raffinement ook kleuraccenten worden aangebracht. Behalve wit kunnen we felle kleuren en klassiekers als hout- en neutrale tinten tegenkomen.

Het meubilair wordt gekenmerkt door rechte lijnen en geometrische vormen. Een badkamer heeft meestal beperkte afmetingen. Een minimalistische stijl verplicht ons tot orde en netheid en zorgt zo voor meer ruimtelijke werking. Tegenwoordig voeren de meeste gespecialiseerde bedrijven modellen voor deze functionele stijl, zonder toeters en bellen.

El minimalismo es uno de los estilos preferidos en el diseño del cuarto de baño. En los baños minimalistas menos es más, salvo cuando se trata de los principales elementos: la luz y el espacio. Los cuartos de baño minimalistas suelen estar hechos de cerámica blanca (para el mobiliario) combinada con el vidrio, el mármol y el acero de los accesorios y con otros elementos como el suelo y las mamparas. Las líneas son limpias y sin adornos.

Este estilo se adapta más a los baños de solteros y parejas, ya que los espacios repletos de objetos, asociados con los baños de familias, se oponen a la estética predominante. Las toallas y otros elementos del baño se guardan en armarios y cajones empotrados, a fin de no interferir con la simetría de ángulos rectos del cuarto.

En la actualidad, los baños pueden diseñarse con una infinidad de materiales. A pesar de que el mármol todavía es el material predominante, sobre todo para baños elegantes, y aunque la piedra y el vidrio han ganado terreno, cuesta imaginar que algún día superen la funcionalidad de las bañeras y los lavabos de cerámica.

El estilo minimalista nos lleva también a espacios diáfanos y monocromáticos, aunque en algunos se imponga una nota de color para aportar un toque de sofisticación. Además del blanco, podemos encontrar colores ácidos y los eternos clásicos como la madera y los tonos neutros.

En lo referente al mobiliario se apuesta por las líneas rectas y los muebles de formas geométricas. Normalmente las dimensiones del cuarto de baño suelen ser reducidas. El estilo minimalista permitirá un plus de amplitud ya que obliga a tener las cosas en orden. Actualmente todas las firmas especializadas cuentan con modelos que encajan con este estilo funcional y despojado de accesorios.

Il minimalismo è uno degli stili leader nel design della stanza da bagno. Nei bagni minimalisti, il meno è più, tranne i casi in cui ci si riferisce agli elementi principali: la luce e lo spazio. I bagni minimalisti sono normalmente fatti con ceramica bianca (per i mobili) combinata con il vetro, il marmo e l'acciaio degli accessori e con altri elementi come il pavimento e i paraventi. Le linee sono pulite e senza ornamenti.

Questo stile si adatta maggiormente ai bagni di single e coppie; infatti, gli spazi colmi di oggetti, associati ai bagni delle famiglie, si oppongono all'estetica predominante. Gli asciugamani e altri oggetti del bagno sono custoditi in armadi e cassetti a muro, al fine di non interferire con la simmetria degli angoli retti della stanza.

Attualmente, i bagni possono essere progettati con un'infinità di materiali. Nonostante il marmo sia ancora il materiale dominante, in particolare per bagni eleganti, e anche se la pietra e il vetro hanno guadagnato terreno, è difficile immaginare che un giorno possano superare la funzionalità delle vasche da bagno e lavabi di ceramica.

Lo stile minimalista ci porta anche a spazi trasparenti e monocromatici, anche se in alcuni s'impone una nota di colore per offrire un tocco di raffinatezza. Oltre al bianco, possiamo trovare colori acidi e i classici senza tempo come il legno e i toni neutri.

Per quanto riguarda l'arredamento si punta sulle linee rette e sui mobili dalle forme geometriche. Normalmente le dimensioni della stanza da bagno sono ridotte. Lo stile minimalista consentirà un plus di grandezza poiché obbliga a tenere le cose in ordine. Al momento, tutte le marche specializzate dispongono di modelli in accordo con questo stile funzionale e privo di accessori.

O minimalismo é um dos estilos que lideram o *design* de banheiros. Nos banheiros minimalistas, o menos é mais, exceto quando se trata dos principais elementos: luz e espaço. Os banheiros minimalistas são normalmente em cerâmica branca (para o mobiliário) combinada com o vidro, o mármore ou o aço dos acessórios e com outros elementos como o piso e os resguardos. As linhas são puras e sem adornos.

Este estilo adapta-se mais aos banheiros de solteiros e de casais sem filhos, uma vez que os espaços repletos de objetos, que caracterizam os banheiros das famílias, ofendem a estética predominante. As toalhas e outros artigos de banho são guardados em armários e gavetas embutidas, para não interferirem com a simetria de ângulos retos da divisão.

Atualmente, podem conceber-se banheiros com uma infinidade de materiais. Embora o mármore continue a ser o material predominante, sobretudo para banheiros elegantes, e a pedra e o vidro tenham vindo a ganhar terreno, é difícil imaginar que algum dia venham a ultrapassar a funcionalidade das banheiras e lavatórios em cerâmica.

O estilo minimalista conduz-nos também a espaços amplos e monocromáticos, embora em alguns se imponha uma nota de cor, que lhes confere um toque sofisticado. Para além do branco, podemos encontrar cores ácidas e os eternos clássicos como a madeira e os tons neutros.

No que se refere ao mobiliário, aposta-se nas linhas retas e nos móveis de formas geométricas. Normalmente, as dimensões do banheiro são reduzidas. O estilo minimalista permite conferir-lhes uma maior amplitude, uma vez que obriga a manter tudo arrumado. Atualmente todas as firmas especializadas contam com modelos que se encaixam bem neste estilo funcional e despojado de acessórios.

Minimalismen är en av de ledande stilarna inom badrumsdesignen. I minimalistiska badrum är ju mindre desto bättre, utom när det gäller det viktigaste: ljus och rymlighet. De minimalistiska badrummen är vanligen inredda i vit keramik (för möblerna) i kombination med glas, marmor och stål för rör och andra detaljer, som golv och skärmar. Linjerna är rena och avskalade.

Den här stilen är mer lämpad för badrum för singlar och par, eftersom badrum som är fullproppade med föremål, som barnfamiljers badrum ofta är, inte stämmer med den estetiken. Handdukar och andra saker förvaras i skåp och lådor, för att inte störa symmetrin i de räta vinklarna.

Idag kan man designa badrummen med en oändlig mängd material. Även om marmor fortfarande är ett vanligt material, speciellt i eleganta badrum, och även sten och glas har vunnit mark, är det svårt att föreställa sig att de någonsin överträffar den så funktionella keramiken för badkar och handfat.

Den minimalistiska stilen ger oss också öppna och monokroma badrum, även om man ofta har ett inslag av färg för att ge en touche av elegans. Utöver vitt stöter man också på starka färger och tidlösa klassiker som trä och neutrala toner.

När det gäller möbler väljer man raka linjer och geometriska former. Oftast är utrymmena för badrum ganska begränsade. Den minimalistiska stilen gör det möjligt att skapa mer utrymme och det tvingar en att hålla ordning. För närvarande har alla specialiserade företag modeller som passar denna funktionella stil och låter en gömma alla tillbehör.

317

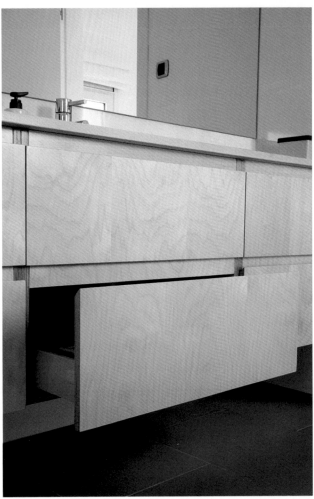

TIPS

© DURAT

The minimalist aesthetic is a sure bet for visually enlarging any space.

La estética minimalista es una apuesta segura para agrandar visualmente cualquier espacio.

Opter pour une esthétique minimaliste est un choix sûr si vous désirez agrandir visuellement un espace.

L'estetica minimalista è una scommessa sicura per aumentare visivamente qualsiasi spazio.

Mit dem minimalistischen Stil lässt sich jeder Raum optisch vergrößern.

A estética minimalista é uma aposta segura para ampliar visualmente qualquer espaço.

Met een minimalistische esthetiek bent u verzekerd van een ruimte die groter oogt dan hij is.

Den minimalistiska stilen är ett säkert kort för att förstora vilket rum som helst.

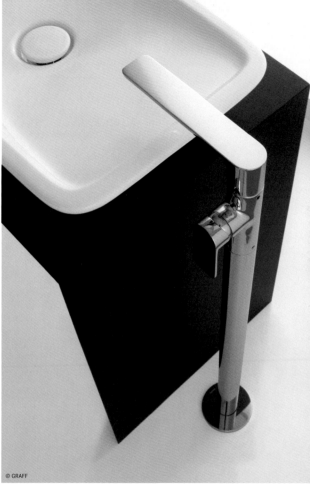

Aim for simplicity and clean lines. Aluminium and steel in their various forms are essential.

Apuesta por la sencillez y las líneas puras. El aluminio y el acero en sus diferentes acabados son imprescindibles.

Faites le choix de la simplicité et des lignes pures. L'aluminium et l'acier aux différents finis sont incontournables.

Punta sulla semplicità e le linee pure. L'alluminio e l'acciaio nelle loro varie finiture sono imprescindibili.

Entscheiden Sie sich für Einfachheit und klare Linien. Aluminium und Stahl in ihren verschiedenen Verarbeitungen sind unerlässlich.

Aposte na simplicidade e nas linhas puras. O alumínio e o aço, com os seus diversos tipos de acabamento, são imprescindíveis.

Wanneer u voor eenvoud en heldere lijnen gaat, zijn aluminium en staal in al hun verschillende verschijningsvormen onmisbaar.

Håll dig till enkla och rena linjer. Aluminium och stål i olika utföranden är ovärderliga.

© CERAMICA CIELO

© CERAMICA CIELO

367

© CERAMICA CIELO

368

© DURAT

A refined look full of straight lines will help you to achieve a clean and natural environment.

Con una depurada imagen de líneas rectas conseguirás un ambiente limpio y sin artificios.

Avec un ensemble épuré tout en lignes droites, vous obtiendrez un environnement clair et dénué d'artifices.

Con un'immagine raffinata dalle linee rette otterrai un ambiente sobrio e senza artifici.

Durch den reinen Aspekt, der durch die geraden Linien erzeugt wird, lässt sich ein klares und ungekünstelt wirkendes Ambiente erzeugen.

Com uma imagem depurada, de linhas retas, vai conseguir um ambiente *clean* e sem artifícios.

Met een spel van zuivere rechte lijnen bent u verzekerd van een heldere en strakke uitstraling.

Med en förfinad yta av raka linjer åstadkommer du en ren och okonstlad miljö.

371

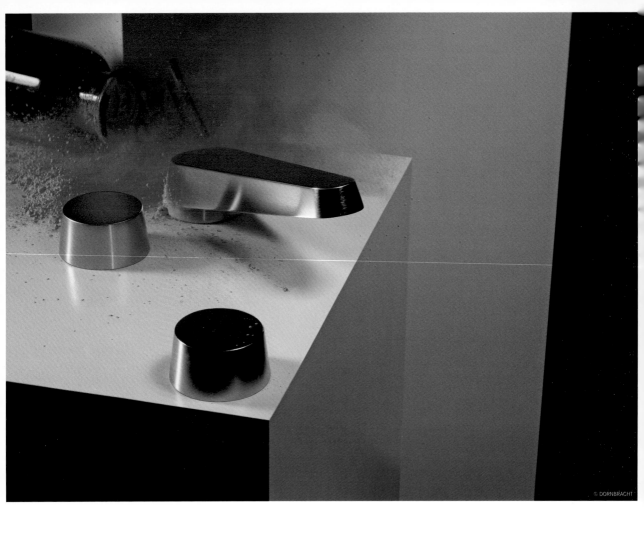

© DORNBRACHT

© CERAMICA CIELO

377

© CERAMICA FLAMINIA

382

© DURAT

Opt for seamless surfaces. The objective is to attain a continuous effect that reinforces the sense of depth.

Opta por revestimientos sin juntas. El objetivo es conseguir un efecto continuo que refuerce la sensación de profundidad.

Optez pour des revêtements sans joints afin d'obtenir un effet de continuité qui renforce l'impression de profondeur.

Scegli rivestimenti senza giunture. L'obiettivo è ottenere un effetto continuo che rinforzi la sensazione di profondità.

Entscheiden Sie sich für Verkleidungen ohne Fugen. Ziel ist es, einen durchgehenden Effekt zu erreichen, der den Eindruck der Schlichtheit verstärkt.

Opte por revestimentos sem juntas. O objetivo é conseguir um efeito de continuidade que reforce a sensação de profundidade.

Kies voor afwerkingslagen zonder naden. Zo realiseert u een doorgaand vlak dat het gevoel van diepte versterkt.

Satsa på sömlösa beläggningar. Målet är att uppnå en kontinuerlig effekt som förstärker känslan av djup.

DURAT

Be careful choosing accessories. Include only the essentials to save space and increase brightness.

Elige los complementos con esmero. Quédate solo con lo esencial y ganarás amplitud y luminosidad.

Choisissez vos accessoires avec soin. Tenez-vous en à l'essentiel, vous y gagnerez en espace et en luminosité.

Scegli gli accessori con cura. Limitati solo all'essenziale e guadagnerai in ampiezza e luminosità.

Wählen Sie Ihre Accessoires mit Bedacht. Entscheiden Sie sich nur für das Nötige. Dies schafft Raum und Helligkeit.

Escolha os acessórios com cuidado. Fique só com o essencial, para ganhar em amplitude e luminosidade.

Kies uw accessoires met zorg. Neem alleen wat echt nodig is om ruimte en licht te winnen.

Välj tillbehör med största omsorg. Behåll bara det nödvändigaste för att vinna rymd och ljus.

393

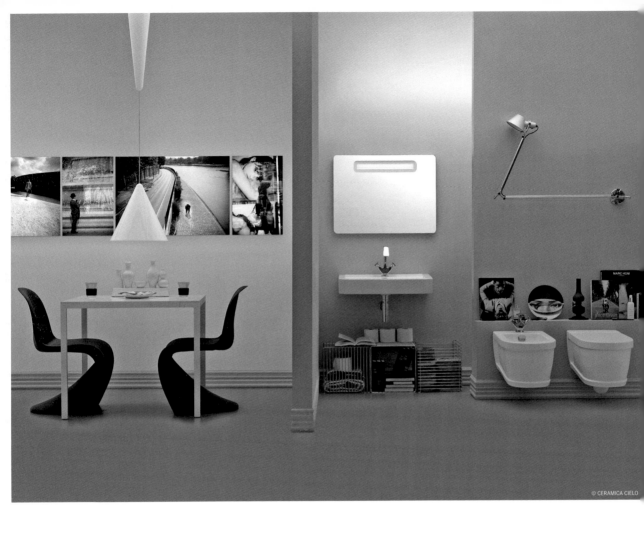

© CERAMICA CIELO

OPEN & ENSUITE BATHROOMS

SALLES DE BAINS OUVERTES ET EN ENFILADE

OFFENE BÄDER UND BÄDER EN SUITE

OPEN BADKAMERS EN BADKAMERS EN SUITE

BAÑOS ABIERTOS Y EN SUITE

BAGNI APERTI E EN SUITE

BANHEIROS ABERTOS E *EN SUITE*

ÖPPNA BADRUM OCH BADRUM I SOVRUMMET

It is increasingly common to find bathrooms integrated into the bedroom, a trend inspired by hotel suites. A bathroom connected to the bedroom may include a sink or even a shower or bathtub. However, it is preferable for the toilet to be located outside of the bedroom in order to avoid unpleasant odours or unnecessary noise in the sleeping quarters.

The advantages of having a sink or shower near the resting area basically have to do with aesthetics and comfort. But it is important to ensure that the bathroom receives good natural light and is well ventilated, or else these advantages can be nullified by a space that is dark and humid. Likewise, it is advisable, whenever possible, to have a nice view from the bathroom window, thus creating a space that is open to the outside world. If the bathroom does not have windows, a greater sense of depth can be achieved with decorative images, such as landscapes.

On the other hand, if you do not want the space to be totally open, you can opt for doors and moving panels, which are a perfect option for keeping both areas open. This makes it possible to have a more private space when necessary.

In these types of spaces, it is recommended that you use natural materials matching the aesthetics of bedroom. This makes it possible to achieve a seamless transition between the two areas that masks the separation between the rooms. Plants can also be used provided if there is sufficient light. What is important is to achieve a harmony of materials and properly decorate the two spaces.

Immer häufiger findet man Bäder vor, die in das Schlafzimmer integriert sind, wobei Hotelsuiten als Vorbild dienen. Ein Bad mit Zugang zum Schlafzimmer kann ein Waschbecken, aber auch Dusche oder Badewanne enthalten. Dennoch befindet sich die Toilette für gewöhnlich außerhalb des Raumes, um schlechte Gerüche oder störende Geräusche daraus zu verbannen.

Die Vorteile, ein Waschbecken oder eine Dusche in der Nähe seines Schlafplatzes zu haben, sind vor allem eine Frage der Ästhetik und des Komforts. Wichtig ist es, sich zu versichern, dass das Bad viel natürliches Licht erhält und gut belüftet ist, damit nicht Dunkelheit und Feuchtigkeit die Vorteile zunichte machen. Wenn möglich, empfiehlt es sich dafür zu sorgen, dass man vom Badfenster aus eine gute Aussicht genießen kann. Dieser Aspekt macht es zu einem nach außen offenen Ort. Wenn das Bad keine Fenster hat, kann anhand dekorativer Bilder das Gefühl von Raumtiefe erzeugt werden. So können beispielsweise Landschaften nachempfunden werden.

Sollte andererseits kein komplett offener Raum gewünscht sein, kann man sich für Türen und bewegliche Wandplatten entscheiden, eine perfekte Möglichkeit für zwei halboffene Räumen. So kann man, wenn nötig, einen sehr intimen Bereich schaffen.

Hier empfiehlt es sich, natürliche Materialien zu verwenden, die mit dem Stil des Schlafzimmers harmonieren. Man versucht für beide Räume eine perfekte Erweiterung zu schaffen, wobei komplett verdeckt wird, dass es sich um zwei getrennte Räume handelt. Bei genügend Licht kann man sich auch für natürliche Pflanzen entscheiden. Es sollte lediglich darauf geachtet werden, dass die Materialien harmonieren und die Dekoration beider Räume übereinstimmt.

Il est toujours plus normal de disposer d'une salle de bain intégrée à la chambre, à la manière des suites d'hôtels. Une salle de bains annexe à la chambre peut comprendre un lavabo et même une douche ou une baignoire. Cependant, il est recommandé d'installer les toilettes en dehors de la chambre pour éviter les mauvaises odeurs ou des bruits intempestifs dans la chambre.

Disposer d'un lavabo ou d'une douche à proximité de l'espace de repos présente surtout un avantage en termes esthétiques et pratiques. Mais il est important de s'assurer que la salle de bains soit bien exposée à la lumière naturelle et bien ventilée, car vous ne gagneriez rien à avoir un espace obscur et humide. En outre, il est recommandé – lorsque cela est possible – de disposer d'une belle vue depuis la fenêtre de la salle de bains afin d'obtenir un espace ouvert sur l'extérieur. Si la salle de bains ne dispose d'aucune fenêtre, il est possible d'apporter à l'espace une impression accrue de profondeur grâce à des images décoratives en perspective qui figurent, par exemple, des paysages.

Par ailleurs, si vous ne désirez pas conserver cet espace totalement ouvert, vous pouvez opter pour des portes et des panneaux mobiles, une solution parfaite pour garder les deux zones comme entr'ouvertes. Ainsi, vous pouvez gagner en intimité dans un espace ou l'autre quand vous le désirez.

Dans ce type d'espaces, il vaut mieux utiliser des matériaux naturels qui se fondent avec l'esthétique de la chambre. Il s'agit d'obtenir un prolongement sans faille d'une zone à l'autre en dissimulant complètement ce qui sépare les deux pièces. Vous pouvez également utiliser des plantes naturelles si vous disposez d'un espace suffisamment lumineux. Il est important de s'assurer que les matériaux et la décoration des deux environnements soient en harmonie.

Steeds vaker zien we badkamers met een open verbinding naar de slaapkamer, geïnspireerd op hotelsuites. Een badkamer *en suite* is meestal voorzien van een wastafel en een bad of douche. Het toilet kan beter ergens anders worden geplaatst, dit om onaangename geuren of ongewenste geluiden in de slaapkamer te voorkomen.

De voordelen van een wastafel of douche dicht bij het rustvertrek hebben voornamelijk te maken met esthetiek en comfort. Het is echter wel van belang dat de badkamer daglicht krijgt of goed geventileerd wordt omdat anders de voordelen teniet worden gedaan en u met een donkere en vochtige ruimte zit. Ook is het aan te bevelen om als dat mogelijk is een raam met uitzicht te plaatsen, waardoor een verbinding met de buitenwereld ontstaat. Als de badkamer geen raam heeft, kunt u met decoratieve afbeeldingen in perspectief, bijvoorbeeld van een landschap, een gevoel van ruimtelijkheid en diepte opwekken.

Als u de ruimte niet helemaal open wilt laten kunt u kiezen voor een deur of schuifpanelen, een uitstekende manier voor een halfopen verbinding tussen beide ruimtes. Zo kunt u eenvoudig meer privacy creëren wanneer dat wenselijk is.

Het is aan te bevelen om in zulke ruimtes natuurlijke materialen te gebruiken die goed passen bij de esthetiek van de slaapkamer. Het doel is namelijk een perfecte aansluiting tussen beide zones te verwezenlijken door de scheiding ertussen zo veel mogelijk op te heffen. Als er voldoende licht is, kunt u ook planten gebruiken. Waar het om gaat is dat zowel de gebruikte materialen als de aankleding van beide vertrekken met elkaar harmoniëren.

Cada vez es más habitual encontrar baños integrados en el dormitorio, inspirados en las suites de los hoteles. Un baño anexo al dormitorio puede incorporar un lavamanos, incluso una ducha o una bañera. Sin embargo, es conveniente que el inodoro se sitúe fuera de la habitación para evitar malos olores o ruidos innecesarios dentro de la habitación.

Las ventajas de tener un lavamanos o una ducha cerca de la zona de descanso se reducen básicamente a cuestiones estéticas y de comodidad, pero es importante asegurarse de que el baño reciba una buena luz natural y esté bien ventilado, ya que si no las ventajas se verán anuladas por tener un espacio oscuro y húmedo. Igualmente, es recomendable, en caso de que sea posible, lograr una vista bonita desde la ventana del baño consiguiendo un espacio abierto al exterior. Si el baño no tiene ventanas se puede crear una mayor sensación de profundidad por medio de imágenes decorativas en perspectiva, por ejemplo creando paisajes.

Por otro lado, si no se quiere dejar el espacio totalmente abierto se puede optar por puertas y paneles móviles, que son una opción perfecta para dejar ambas zonas entreabiertas. De esta manera, se puede conseguir un área más íntima en caso de que sea necesario.

En este tipo de espacios se recomienda utilizar materiales naturales que se integren con la estética del dormitorio. Se trata de conseguir una prolongación perfecta entre ambas zonas disimulando por completo la separación de las habitaciones. También se puede optar por usar plantas naturales si se dispone de la suficiente luz. Lo importante es acertar tanto en la armonía de los materiales como en la decoración de los dos ambientes.

È sempre più comune trovare bagni inclusi nella stanza da letto, ispirati alle suite degli hotel. Un bagno annesso alla camera può includere un lavabo, e addirittura una doccia o una vasca da bagno. Tuttavia, è preferibile che il water sia collocato fuori dalla stanza per evitare cattivi odori o rumori inopportuni all'interno della camera.

I vantaggi di avere un lavandino o una doccia vicino alla zona di riposo si riducono essenzialmente a questioni estetiche e di comodità. È comunque importante assicurarsi che il bagno riceva una buona luce naturale e sia ben ventilato, altrimenti i vantaggi saranno annullati da uno spazio scuro e umido. È anche raccomandabile, se possibile, assicurarsi una bella vista dalla finestra del bagno, ottenendo uno spazio aperto sull'esterno. Se il bagno non dispone di finestre, è possibile creare una maggiore sensazione di profondità tramite immagini decorative in prospettiva, ad esempio dando vita a paesaggi.

D'altra parte, se non si vuole lasciare lo spazio completamente aperto, è possibile optare per porte e pannelli mobili, che rappresentano una scelta perfetta per lasciare entrambe le zone semiaperte. In questo modo, è possibile ottenere una zona più intima in caso di bisogno.

In questo genere di spazi si raccomanda l'utilizzo di materiali naturali che si integrino nell'estetica della stanza da letto. Si tratta di ottenere un prolungamento perfetto tra le due zone, nascondendo completamente la separazione delle stanze. È anche possibile prediligere l'utilizzo di piante naturali, nel caso in cui la luce sia sufficiente. L'importante è fare la scelta giusta sia per quanto riguarda l'armonia dei materiali sia per l'arredamento dei due ambienti.

É cada vez mais habitual encontrar banheiros integrados no quarto, inspirados nas suítes dos hotéis. Um banheiro anexo ao quarto pode incluir um lavatório e até mesmo uma ducha ou uma banheira. No entanto, é conveniente que o sanitário fique fora do quarto, para evitar maus cheiros ou ruídos desnecessários dentro do quarto.

As vantagens de ter um lavatório ou uma ducha próximo da área de repouso reduzem-se basicamente a questões estéticas e de conforto. É, no entanto, importante garantir que o banheiro receba uma boa luz natural e seja bem ventilado, caso contrário, as vantagens serão anuladas, resultando num espaço escuro e húmido. É igualmente aconselhável, sempre que possível, ter uma vista bonita da janela do banheiro, para conseguir um espaço virado para o exterior. Se o banheiro não tiver janela, pode-se criar uma sensação de maior profundidade por meio de imagens decorativas em perspetiva, por exemplo, com paisagens.

Por outro lado, se não se pretende deixar o espaço totalmente aberto, pode-se optar por portas e painéis móveis, que constituem uma opção perfeita para deixar ambas as zonas entreabertas. Desta maneira, consegue-se, caso seja necessário, uma maior privacidade.

Neste tipo e espaços recomenda-se a utilização de materiais naturais que se integrem na estética do quarto. Trata-se de conseguir um prolongamento perfeito entre ambas as zonas, dissimulando completamente a separação entre elas. Também se pode optar pelo uso de plantas naturais, se se dispuser de luz suficiente. O importante é acertar tanto na harmonia dos materiais como na decoração dos dois ambientes.

Det blir allt vanligare att integrera badrum i sovrummen, med hotellen som förebild. Ett badrum i sovrummet kan innehålla ett handfat och kanske även en dusch eller ett badkar. Det är ändå bäst att placera toaletten utanför rummet för att slippa obehagliga lukter och ljud i rummet.

Fördelarna med att ha ett handfat eller en dusch nära sängen är framför allt utseende och bekvämlighet. Men det är viktigt att se till att badrummet får bra dagsljus och är väl ventilerat, annars kommer nackdelarna att överväga över fördelarna, med ett mörkt och fuktigt rum. Det är också klokt, om möjligt, att försöka få till en fin utsikt från badrumsfönstret med en öppen yta utanför. Saknar badrummet fönster kan man skapa en större känsla av djup genom dekorativa perspektivbilder, som till exempel landskap.

Om man inte vill lämna utrymmet vidöppet kan man välja flyttbara dörrar och paneler, som är ett perfekt val för att öppna upp mellan utrymmena. På det sättet kan man göra rummet mer intimt när man så önskar.

I den typen av rum rekommenderas att man använder naturliga material som passar ihop med stilen i sovrummet. Det handlar om att få till en perfekt förlängning mellan de båda zonerna, som helt döljer gränsen mellan rummen. Man kan också välja att använda levande växter om det finns tillräckligt med ljus. Det viktigaste är att ta hänsyn till harmonin, både mellan materialen och dekoren i de två miljöerna.

425

431

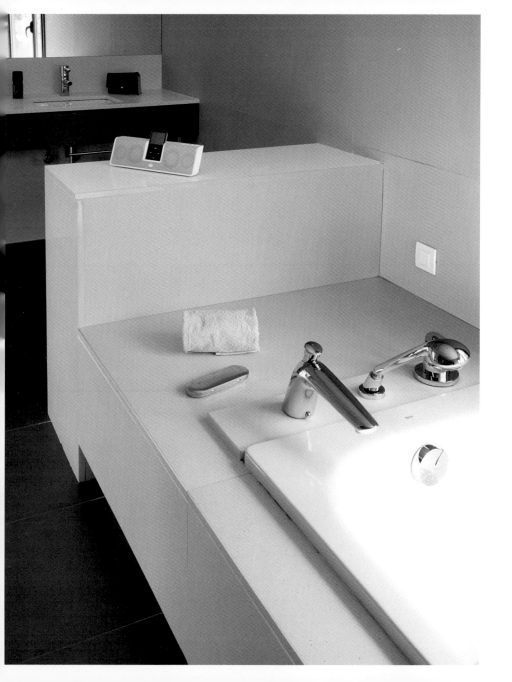

451

471

TIPS

© NEUTRA

APARICI

Getting up in the morning and brushing your teeth while contemplating the scenery can be the best way to wake up your body and mind.

Levantarse por la mañana y lavarse los dientes contemplando el paisaje puede ser la mejor forma de despertar el cuerpo y la mente.

Se lever le matin et se laver les dents en admirant le paysage : n'est-ce pas là la meilleure manière de réveiller son corps et son esprit ?

Alzarsi al mattino e lavarsi i denti guardando il paesaggio può essere il modo migliore per svegliare corpo e mente.

Morgens erwachen und beim Zähneputzen die Landschaft betrachten ist mitunter die beste Möglichkeit, Körper und Geist zu wecken.

Levantar-se de manhã e escovar os dentes contemplando a paisagem pode ser a melhor forma de despertar o corpo e a mente.

's Ochtends opstaan en uw tanden poetsen met uitzicht op het landschap is waarschijnlijk de beste manier voor lichaam en geest om te ontwaken.

Att kunna stiga upp på morgonen och njuta av utsikten samtidigt som man borstar tänderna kan vara det bästa sättet att väcka både kropp och sinne.

© APARICI

A solution for this type of mixed space could be customized walls or changes of level. Furniture can be the perfect way of joining the two spaces.

Una solución para este tipo de espacios mixtos son los muros a medida o los cambios de nivel. El mobiliario puede ser una opción perfecta para unir ambos ambientes.

Pour ce genre d'espaces mixtes, l'une des solutions consiste à ériger des murets ou opter pour des dénivelés. Le mobilier représente un moyen parfait de relier la chambre et la salle de bains.

Una soluzione per questo tipo di spazi misti sono i muri su misura o i cambi di livello. I mobili possono essere una scelta perfetta per unire i due ambienti.

Trennwände und der Ebenenwechsel sind eine ideale Lösung für diese kombinierten Räume. Mit dem Mobiliar lassen sich beide Räume perfekt verbinden.

Uma solução para este tipo de espaços mistos são os muros sob medida e as diferenças de nível. O mobiliário pode ser uma opção perfeita para ligar ambos os ambientes.

Voor dit type gemengde ruimtes is een muur op maat of een hoogteverschil een oplossing. Beide ruimtes kunnen met meubels uitstekend met elkaar worden verbonden.

En lösning för den här typen av kombinerat rum är rumsavskiljande halvväggar eller nivåskillnader. Möblerna kan vara perfekta för att koppla ihop de båda miljöerna.

483

© TAU CERÁMICA

In bathrooms with a view, it is always advisable to have blinds or curtains for privacy at any given time.

En los baños con vistas es siempre aconsejable tener unos estores o cortinas por si queremos intimidad en algún momento.

Dans les salles de bains avec vue, il est recommandé d'avoir des stores ou des rideaux si vous aspirez à plus d'intimité à un moment donné.

Nei bagni con vista è sempre consigliabile avere tende a pacchetto o normali nel caso in cui desideriamo un momento di privacy.

Für den Fall, dass Diskretion gewünscht ist, empfehlen sich für offene Bäder Gardinen oder Stores.

Nos banheiros com vista é sempre aconselhável ter persianas ou cortinas, para o caso de em algum momento querer ter mais privacidade.

In een badkamer met uitzicht is een (rol)gordijn aan te bevelen voor de momenten waarop privacy gewenst is.

I badrum med utsikt är det alltid klokt att ha persienner eller gardiner för att få avskildhet när så önskas.

493

494

© BURGBAD BATH INNOVATIONS

Don't give up the idea of putting your bathtub next to a window if you live in the city. If you live on the top floor, you can install Velux® windows on the roof above the bathtub.

No renuncies a colocar tu bañera junto a una ventana aunque vivas en una ciudad. Si vives en un ático puedes abrir unas ventanas Velux® en el tejado sobre la bañera.

Si vous vivez en ville, ne renoncez pas à placer votre baignoire près de la fenêtre. Si vous vivez dans les combles, vous pouvez installer quelques Velux® au plafond au-dessus de la baignoire.

Non rinunciare a sistemare la tua vasca da bagno vicino ad una finestra se vivi in città. Se vivi in un attico, puoi aprire delle finestre Velux® nel tetto sopra alla vasca da bagno.

Wenn Sie in der Stadt leben, sollten Sie nicht darauf verzichten, Ihre Badewanne unter das Fenster zu stellen. Wenn Sie im Dachgeschoss leben, können Sie Velux®-Dachfenster über der Badewanne anbringen.

Se vive na cidade, não renuncia a colocar a banheira junto a uma janela. Se viver numa mansarda, pode instalar janelas Velux® no telhado, por cima da banheira.

In een stad wonen betekent niet dat het bad niet bij een raam kan staan. Woont u op een zolderverdieping, dan kunt u boven het bad Velux®ramen laten installeren.

Låt dig inte lockas till att placera badkaren vid fönstret om du bor i en stad. Om du har en vindsvåning kan du sätta in Velux®-fönster i taket över badkaret.

© CERAMICA CIELO

501

© TOSCOQUATTRO

DIRECTORY OF BRANDS

Aparici
www.aparici.com

Apavisa Porcelánico
www.apavisa.com

Boxart
www.boxart.org

Burgbad Bath Innovations
www.burgbad.com

Ceramica Cielo
www.ceramicacielo.it

Ceramica Flaminia
www.ceramicaflaminia.it

Devon & Devon
www.devon-devon.com

Durat
www.durat.com

Graff
www.graff-faucets.com

IB Rubinetterie
www.ibrubinetterie.com

Inda
www.inda.net

Kohler
www.kohler.com

Neutra
www.neutradesign.it

Oceanside
www.glasstile.com

Porcelanosa Grupo
www.porcelanosa.com

Stone Forest
www.stoneforest.com

Tau Cerámica
www.tauceramica.com

Toscoquattro
www.toscoquattro.it

Wetstyle
www.wetstyle.ca